SPEAK
CONNECT
SUCCEED

Build your Reputation As You Speak

Aletta Rochat

ISBN-13: 978-1973733188
ISBN-10: 1973733188

www.voicingyourpotential.com
For orders, please email: aletta.rochat@gmail.com

Dedication

To my children,

Nicole, Cate, and Trevor

I started off my journey as a mother thinking I knew a few things. Each of you has helped me see the world differently and has challenged me to grow.

Thank you for enriching my life beyond measure.

Acknowledgments

Many people along the way have encouraged me to write this book:

My husband, Rory, is my greatest supporter. My children, Nicole, Cate, and Trevor keep reminding me I should just do it.

Many of my Toastmasters community—especially Gao Molebalwa and Njabulo Thela—who offered to buy a copy before it was even written. I have also been blessed to work with many leaders who inspire me, like Craig and Lois Strachan, Erich Viedge, Merryl Jubber, and Craig Valentine.

I have learned a great deal from my clients - thank you for being willing to try new approaches. Most importantly, thank you for sharing your success stories with me.

Beverly Asante, my accountability partner at Self-Publishing School. It has been a privilege to work with you and to be inspired by you. Meeting you in Zurich was a wonderful bonus.

To the many generous people who volunteered to be part of my launch team - thank you for your support and encouragement. Thank you to the Self-Publishing School community for their constant advice and support.

I am fortunate to have inspiring friends who showed me how to publish books, like Lois Strachan and Bronwyn Hesketh. And to all those who have heard me speak and attended my workshops, I'm grateful for your inspiration and feedback. Your voices are reflected in this book. Your contribution is invaluable. Your support encourages me to continue to share my ideas.

Thank you to Cate Rochat for designing my book cover.

Contents

Introduction

Why this Matters to Me
and Why this Matters to You

By the age of eight, I had already learned the value and necessity of speaking well. For me, it had become part of a survival mechanism. I had a very nomadic childhood. My father, Emil, worked in the mining industry. He became a specialist shaft sinker. This unique skill set meant that he was in demand all over the world.

My childhood was a blur of new homes, new towns, cities, and schools. My schooling career started off in South Africa, and subsequently moved to various locations in Zambia, Canada, Tasmania, and then back to South Africa. Every move involved settling into a new house, a new school, and a new world.

From a young age I learned the value of making sure that I integrated into my new environment quickly. As much as I loved my two brothers and my sister, I needed to make friends wherever I was. I needed to have friends of my own to play with. This nomadic childhood was also very demanding. It takes a lot of time and energy to settle into a new community. No sooner had we put down some roots and made friends than we were off to the next place.

Standing in front of yet another new classroom full of strangers, my eight-year-old self understood the rules of the game. In this new environment, I knew that my speaking and my ability to engage with others would determine how quickly I settled. I had already discovered that my words and my ability to listen were vital to settling in well. My speaking would, to a large extent, dictate whether or not I would make friends, whether I would be welcomed into friendship circles, and (crucially, to an eight-year-old) whether I would be invited to birthday parties.

Just as easily, my speaking had the potential to keep me an outsider. I was already the new kid, the one that spoke a different language to that of my classmates, the one who had a funny accent. Those were obvious challenges I had to overcome. If my speaking and communication skills were not effective, I had very little chance of settling in happily.

I moved many more times as both a child and an adult. During these later transitions, I may have been older, and hopefully wiser, but the challenges were the same. When you move into a new environment, you need other people far more than they need you. Our basic human need to interact with other people is as important to an adult as it is to a child. The speaking strategies I had learned by the age of eight have stood the test of time.

I have been able to successfully integrate into new communities all over the world as an adult. And I have consistently— and successfully—applied the same strategies to the workplace. Settling into a new workplace is exceptionally demanding. You need to engage and integrate with your colleagues, not to mention any external clients or customers. (In every situation, there is always someone to please, to influence or to persuade.) The sooner you can do this, the sooner you can become fully effective in your new role. Over and over again, I proved that being able to speak and connect opens doors and acts as a catalyst for opportunity and success.

When you speak with purpose, relevance, and passion, your words become catalysts for opportunity.

As a leader, both in the volunteer space as well as in the business world, I put these strategies to the test. From time to time, people would compliment me on my speaking and leadership style. This feedback was flattering, but I also found it to be confusing. I was receiving compliments and yet I didn't quite understand what I was doing right. My actions were 'obvious' to me—my expectation was that anyone else in the same position would make the same choices. I soon realised that this wasn't the case. I wanted to understand exactly what people were responding to, so I started to ask for more specific feedback. In the process, I discovered that much of what I did innately didn't come so naturally to others. I came to the realization that my nomadic childhood had taught me invaluable lessons. The skills and techniques I had learned and applied during those early years of moving from school to school and country to country had resulted in positive outcomes in my adult life—in the business world, in my personal relationships, and in the volunteer community.

Most importantly, I learned and proved that my ability to speak with purpose was a huge asset. I was able to motivate and inspire individuals and teams, many of whom I had little opportunity to interact with face-to-face. Those teams achieved remarkable results. By continually working on my ability to stand out when I speak up, I learned to get a message through, instead of merely sharing information. I learned to immediately connect with individuals in ways that encouraged them to take action. I learned to speak in ways that people remembered. As a result, I have been hired to speak, coach, and train professionally, both locally and internationally. The majority of my clients are repeat clients. Virtually all of my clients have come to me through recommendations from others. By taking care to speak and connect both positively and personally with clients and colleagues, I have been able to contribute to their learning and success. At the same time, I have been able to grow my network, business and brand.

Communication is a natural part of our lives, and speaking is something many of us do daily and often without thinking. And yet, the consequences of our words can be profound. When you speak, you can change the mood of a room—for better or for worse. Your words might inspire someone to believe in his or her ability. Your words can open up opportunities for you to enhance your reputation. Just as easily though, your words can showcase your vulnerabilities or ruin your or someone else's day.

As you speak, you can engineer your future career prospects or guarantee your own swift exit. Your speaking will identify which kind of leader you are and whether people want you on their team. Your speaking will determine whether or not you stand out from the crowd. When you master the art of speaking with purpose, doors will open up for you that you may never have imagined were within your reach.

This book will take you on a journey to ensure your speaking enhances your reputation at all times, rather than detracts from it. Your speaking will build your brand and increase your presence and influence. Your speaking will connect you with those you are speaking to, in ways that are meaningful to them. In the process, you uncover a greater ability to achieve your goals. Your speaking will allow you to speak, connect and succeed.

Speaking is a means to an end—a way to give instruction, to ask for help, to express emotion, or to give thanks. Rarely do we take a moment to realise the impact of our words.

I am confident that you, like me, have sometimes spoken words in anger, without thinking. Almost as soon as the words leave your mouth, you're already regretting saying them. Then follows the awkward apology, the 'trying to set things right' conversation.

How often have you spoken in a work-related context and felt you haven't quite done justice to yourself, your company, or your personal brand? Perhaps your comments were un-structured, too wordy or not convincing. Maybe you rambled on and on? After the event, it's so easy to think of the perfect points you wish you'd made, but finding them in the moment is a lot more challenging. Think of a phone conversation that didn't go well—when the other person simply didn't get it. Or remember sending that email where your wording wasn't clear and someone either took offence or misinterpreted your words. These scenarios feel all too familiar to far too many of us.

Speaking is every word you say, every email, text, or message you send—every conversation you have.

What if I could show you a way to stand out when you speak up? A simple way of realising the impact of your words and harnessing their potential. Speaking is every word you say, every email, text, or message you send—every conversation you have. Speaking goes way beyond your formal presenta-tions in front of an audience. If you add all those little bits of speaking together, you can start to appreciate the impact of your speaking is far bigger than you may be aware of.

When you put all those little opportunities together and use them purposefully, your voice can have impact and change the status quo. Your voice and your speaking can attract opportunity to you. Once you become skilled at leveraging these everyday opportunities, you will be in a position to get ahead. You will be well ahead of most people, and you will be way ahead of your competition.

Once you realise the pervasiveness of your speaking, you will be aware of the tremendous potential you have to use your voice purposefully. The tips and techniques I will share with you are practical and easy to use. You will be able to speak, connect and succeed once you put them into action. The result? Your speaking will have the potential to build your reputation, to enhance your brand, and to increase your presence and influence. Your speaking will connect with others in ways that are meaningful to them. In the process, you have a greater ability to achieve your goals.

The fact that you are reading this book means that you are one of the enlightened people who want to develop their speaking skills. You want to stand out from the crowd, and putting these principles into practice can get you there. You will be the one that is noticed (for the right reasons!), remembered, and hired. Whether you are a professional speaker, an entrepreneur promoting your business, or a volunteer, you will benefit from what I have to share with you. Once you master these skills, people will respond more positively to you, your message, and your call to action. You'll enhance your ability to connect and engage with others. You will become the person others want to associate with, learn from, and hire. In short, you will soon be speaking your way into opportunity!

All this is available to you when you recognize your own potential. You have the ability to speak and connect in a way that inspires both yourself and others. You can learn the art of speaking purposefully so that you achieve your dreams. You can be the speaker who changes the mood of a room in a positive way, who inspires teams to achieve remarkable results. Your speaking can leave a legacy that lives on beyond you. My greatest wish is that you become the person whose speaking allows you to stand out from the crowd. I am excited to share this knowledge and experience with you.

What is the cost of inaction? You can continue without these skills—no problem—but you would be doing yourself a disservice. It reminds me of an advertising campaign many years ago with the tagline: 'You can stay as you are for the rest of your life…. Or you can change to (Name of Brand).' The choice is yours. Think how many times a day you speak. If you can use that speaking to get ahead, you can enhance your prospects multiple times a day.

Chapter 1

Why Speaking Up is Such a Big Deal, and Why Standing Out is Essential

You might be wondering what all the fuss is about. If we all speak so much every day, surely we already know all there is to know about speaking. Most of us can speak easily, without too much effort. However, it is about far more than saying words. Speaking is about making your voice heard—about making a difference with your words. In the process, you can influence change, inspire, and motivate. Your speaking can literally change your career prospects and become a catalyst for opportunity. The choice is yours—carry on as you have always done, or learn to leverage your speaking to get ahead.

When I refer to 'speaking', I am considering much more than simply the vocalising of words. Speaking is everything you do to communicate with someone else. This includes all of your emails, text messages, social media posts, and even your tweets. Any form of communication is your 'voice.' My definition of speaking also includes your ability to listen. Any moment when you are communicating with someone else, you are speaking. When my daughter tells me she has 'spoken' to her friend, she means she has sent a digital message. Digital words and conversations are just as powerful as spoken words and conversations. Once you grasp how pervasive your speaking is, you will begin to appreciate the multiple oppor-

tunities you have to make your speaking more purposeful—
to connect and succeed.

If you want to get ahead, develop your speaking skills. This investment of time and energy will pay dividends in every aspect of your life.

Why do you need to make your voice heard?

Every single day, you and I have opportunities to make our voices heard. This doesn't have to be saved for those 'big' occasions like presenting in front of hundreds of people or being interviewed by media. You can make your voice heard every time you speak—every time you talk on the phone, send a message, or post on social media. When you put all these little opportunities together and use them purposefully, your voice can have impact and change the status quo. Your voice and your speaking can attract opportunity to you. Once you become skilled at leveraging these everyday opportunities, you will be in a position to get ahead. You will be well ahead of most people, and you will be way ahead of your competition. If you are serious about getting ahead in your career, start today!

Whatever your role, it is vital that you speak up! Whoever hired you needs to know that you are there. This may sound obvious, but it is a fundamental truth. If you have been hired to do a job, you need to let those around you know that you are there doing the job. More importantly, you need to let others know that you are excelling at what you do.

When I first started working, it took me a while to figure this out. I assumed that those around me would see the good work I was doing day after day. Perhaps I thought they were psychic! I certainly thought that they would notice (and of course appreciate) all the work I was quietly doing in my office. This was a mistake—one that was brought painfully to my attention during a performance review. My boss told me he was not getting the same quality of work from me as he was from another person on the same level. I was incensed! I knew that I was working hard. I was outraged that he didn't see and acknowledge my contribution. Of course, at the time, I put all the blame on him.

Once I calmed down, I realised that his perception was based on the fact that he was not hearing my voice. I was not speaking up. I was doing the work but not sharing this and discussing this with him. I was working in isolation. What I didn't understand at that time was that many others needed the reassurance that I was on top of my job. Others needed constant updates on my progress. I was part of a team. Team members collaborate and cooperate.

If you want to thrive in your role, make your voice heard—learn to stand out when you speak up.

Making your voice heard validates the decision your boss made to hire you in the first place. Speaking up lets those around you know that they can rely on you—that things are on track. Speaking up tells your boss that you are earning your keep. Perhaps I should add a word of caution here. For the sake of your reputation, avoid being that person who speaks all the time without adding any value. Simply speaking up at a meeting to hear the sound of your own voice will damage your reputation. You will not be taken seriously. Later in this book, you will learn how to be purposeful about your speaking. It is all about the quality of what you say rather than the quantity of your words. Less (of high quality) is definitely more!

When employers look to promote someone, they want to make the right decision. It's very costly to appoint the wrong person to a role. You might be given a little leeway and time to find your feet. But you are less likely to be promoted or hired if you don't speak up. Your senior management or potential client is looking for reassurance that you are the right person for the job. Everyday speaking opportunities, used well, provide that reassurance.

One of the simplest ways to demonstrate your value is to stand out when you speak up.

What Stops us Speaking Up?

The most obvious reason we don't speak up is that we **lack self-confidence**. I recently met with John, a client of mine. He was a highly qualified engineer who had recently been promoted. He was soft-spoken and also an introvert. John shared with me that he rarely spoke up in meetings. Everyone else spoke up and shot from the hip. In contrast, John sat there and thought about the issues. He liked to think and consider matters before speaking up. John knew he had the knowledge and could add value, but meanwhile his lack of confidence held him back and kept him silent. The result was that his voice was seldom heard. The fact that he prepared well for meetings and came prepared to add value was not that evident to the others. His efforts were, to a certain extent, invisible due to his lack of self-confidence and his habit of not speaking up. On one hand, he was unlikely to be noticed, as his voice was not being heard. On the other hand, he now had a team that reported to him and kept looking to him for leadership. He wasn't able to seize that opportunity. John assumed that they knew what to do, and that they should get on with it. He assumed they didn't need to hear his voice telling them what to do.

John needed to work on developing his self-confidence so that he could make his voice heard in meetings. He needed to learn how to develop the voice of a leader. The good news is that this is not difficult to do. Once you have the right mindset and self-awareness, you can make quick progress. I am happy to report that after we worked on some speaking strategies together, John solved this issue very quickly and effectively. He was markedly more confident when he reported very positive results at our next meeting. He went further and started making his voice heard outside of meetings. He developed the habit of greeting everyone in his department personally every morning. At first they didn't know what to make of this. They were not used to having a leader who took personal interest in the members of the team. But before long, he said they were waiting for him to come and greet them. This was a simple task that allowed him to develop relationships with his team. He used everyday conversations to increase his influence and to achieve his goals. John was speaking up and connecting. This helped him succeed in his new role.

Another reason we don't speak up is that **we don't like to ask for help or feedback**. I fall into this category and avoid asking for help and feedback like the plague. I prefer to figure things out myself and to work independently. In some instances this character trait is positive, but in others it doesn't serve me well. I have wasted an inordinate amount of time figuring it out myself. In my experience, the vast majority of people are very willing to help and provide feedback. Many are even flattered to be asked for advice. My fear of asking for help was hindering my progress! Becoming a Toastmaster helped me overcome this fear. The Toastmasters model encourages everyone to have a mentor. I have often consulted my mentors, Craig and Lois, when I was stuck, had high levels of frustration, or simply needed someone to bounce ideas off. Having outside input allowed me to gain a perspective I could not have gained on my own. I also felt supported. I got through some very challenging times with the help of mentors. They allowed me a safe space to vent my frustrations. After that, I could return to my challenges and speak as an adult rather than an angry, impulsive child. I will forever be grateful for their guidance and friendship.

I suggest asking someone you trust and respect to be your mentor. Meet with them on a regular basis to get advice and feedback on your progress. Clearly define, recognise, and celebrate your strengths as well as areas for improvement. So often we are hyper-aware of our weaknesses, so much so that we don't recognise what others see in us. If someone gives you a compliment, thank them and then ask for specific feedback. Ask the questions that will show you how others see you. Ask for feedback on your speaking. Is your voice being heard? If so, what are you telling others? Analyse whether you are making the most of everyday speaking opportunities.

Become aware of what you do naturally that works. Not every person can do what you do. This innate ability is part of what will allow you to stand out when you speak up. Consider which areas need to be developed. Awareness is always the first step to being able to improve a skill. I was always quite proud of the fact that I didn't have many *um*s and *ah*s when I present. One evening at a Toastmasters meeting, the Grammarian pointed out to me that while I had no *um*s and *ah*s in my speech, I had a grand total of fourteen *now*s! I was totally unaware that I started many sentences with the word *now*, and I was so grateful for that feedback. Once I became aware of this, I was able to start working on eliminating this from my speaking. Awareness is the first step towards improvement. Your mentor can give you this feedback in a positive way— along with suggestions for improvement.

You might hesitate to speak up because **you don't feel like you can add value.** This is closely tied to lack of confidence. Experience has taught me that you can add value no matter how high up or low down you are on the food chain. You don't need to have the corner office to be able to add value. Your observation and contribution from anywhere in an office or a committee can be profound.

A few years ago, I was about to go into theatre for a medical procedure. Naturally I was a bit nervous. One of the hospital porters came up to me, looked me in the eye, smiled, and said: 'Mrs Rochat, we are going to take *very* good care of you.' His words were just what I needed at that time! He didn't have a medical degree, he wasn't going to be in the theatre, but he understood that he could add value when he spoke up. His focus was on reassuring patients, and he did that exceptionally well. In fact, he reassured me far more than my surgeon did! He added tremendous value with a few simple words, spoken authentically. Whatever your contribution in an organisation or to a process, you can add value. Your opinions and perspectives need to be heard. Your suggestion could be the one that makes a difference, that solves a problem, or that provides opportunity. You are a vital link in the chain!

Perhaps you hesitate to speak up as you **don't think it will make a difference.** That is often a reason people don't vote in elections—they come to the conclusion that their vote won't make any difference. One of my favourite authors, Mike Dooley, in his book *Leveraging the Universe*, says: 'Do what you can with what you have from where you are.' Don't wait for circumstances to be perfect before you take action and speak up. You and I cannot always predict when our words will make a difference, which of our words others will remember. Many times we do speak and we don't immediately see the difference that those words make. My advice is to simply speak and strive to add value. Let go of the outcome. Simply get in the habit of speaking up. How else can you influence change and try and improve the status quo?

You and I need to speak up for what is right. So much oppression, corruption, and bullying thrives when people stay silent. It is not always easy to speak up under these circumstances. There are situations when your speaking up for what is right will bring negative consequences, either at home, in the community, or in the workplace. Despite the consequences, there often comes a time when you can no longer stay silent. You will know when this happens and will find the courage to do this. Speaking up for what is right doesn't have to be a voice on a public platform. It can be a quiet voice in a private conversation. If you can't speak to the bully, then speak to someone who can give you advice on how to cope with the situation you are facing. This is not a book to help you cope with drastic situations when you are being oppressed or bullied. However, the principles I am sharing with you will help you speak up for what is right.

What Happens when you get it Right? If you are the one who stands out when you speak up, you will be in a position to increase your influence, your presence, and the impact you have. This is true for you as an individual and for you as a team, a brand or a company. You will attract opportunity to yourself by adding value when you speak. Later in this book we will go into more detail on how to achieve this.

What Happens when you get it Wrong? You can feel it! There is no connection and no response to your speaking. At worst, there is a negative response. It is painful and often impossible to come back from a negative response. No response is almost as bad. Often what happens is that we blame the other party. *They* must be the problem. Then we go and speak to the next prospect and get the same result again. Once again, we blame *them*. In the meantime, we see our sales decrease, we don't close deals, our reputation is tarnished. Sometimes you can see money going to someone else instead of to you. It's as if the opportunity vanishes before your eyes. If you recognise any of these scenarios, keep reading! The solutions to these problems are waiting for you in the chapters that follow. If you speak up without adding value, you can easily become an irritation to others. If you speak up with no regard for the time you take, you end up wasting everyone else's time.

If you speak up and insist on only speaking about an issue relevant to you, you become someone others don't want to work with. Your speaking happens in a context, and it should add value to the meeting, to the discussion, and to the team. Your speaking shouldn't dominate or overpower others. Your speaking must honour the timeframe you are given. Your speaking should be relevant to the others at that meeting.

We live in a competitive world. Whatever you do, many others are probably doing something similar. What makes you stand out from the rest? Often your products or services or talents are very similar to those of your competitor. If you are the one who stands out when you speak up, you can make it easier for someone to choose you.

When you are articulate and purposeful with your speaking, you inspire confidence. People do business with people they know, like, and trust. If you speak up and connect, you increase the likelihood that someone will choose to work with you. To thrive in this world, you need to be the one to stand out. It is not that complicated. All you need to do is to connect with your audience. The next chapter will show you proven ways to connect.

Chapter 2

Seven Proven Ways to Speak and Connect

It is not especially complicated to connect with your audience, but that doesn't mean it's easy to do. If it was, you would never have to listen to a boring speaker droning on and on. If it was easy to do, you would be spared the agony of listening to a speaker you can't relate to, perhaps one that confuses you. If connecting with your audience was easy to do, you'd never have to cope with the results of a bad presentation. I have experienced that, and it is not an experience I want to repeat.

Many years ago, I was marketing a product. I decided to use presentations to service organisations as a tool to generate leads and sell products. I studied the material, memorised the prepared presentation given to me, and set up a speaking opportunity. The alarm bells should have been ringing loudly in my ears by then. I was using a presentation written by someone I had never met, someone who was from a different country and culture than I am. I was speaking someone else's words and thoughts. Polite applause followed the end of my presentation. Someone stood up to thank me, and I will never forget his words: "Thank you Aletta. I had no idea what you were talking about. Thank you."

I was mortified. Looking back, it was obvious that I hadn't connected with the audience at all. The presentation was all about me and what I was trying to sell, and not about the audience or their needs or interests. It was a painful, public lesson on what *not* to do when presenting.

I hope you never have to go through an experience like this. The good news is that connecting isn't so difficult when you become aware of how important it is and what tactics might work best to align your experience with your audience's. This chapter will help increase your awareness and offer practical tactics by showing you seven proven ways to connect:

1. Connect by Listening & Observing Intently

It All Starts with Listening. Would you be surprised to learn that the first step to connecting is to listen? Does it seem counter-intuitive that you can make a good impression before you even say one word? Perhaps you can remember situations when you spoke endlessly, rambling on and on because you were nervous. I know I have done that on many an occasion. Isn't it strange how often we find ourselves deeply uncomfortable with silence?

For those of us who are introverts (and I am definitely one of you), it is a relief to realise that we don't need to dominate conversation to stand out. We all know someone who speaks without adding any value. It seems that person is in love with his or her own voice. His conversation doesn't even require an audience, because so often it is a stream of consciousness relevant only to him. Don't be that person!

One of my favourite books is *The Charisma Myth* by Olivia Fox Cabane. She was the one who introduced me to the concept of charismatic listening. Whatever you may think of Bill Clinton, he was well known for being a superb listener and making the person he was talking to feel like the most important person in the world. To quote Olivia Fox Cabane: 'Think of how you would behave if you were indeed speaking to the most important person in the room. You would probably want to hear everything they had to say. You'd be truly interested, maybe even impressed, and that attitude is exactly what will make people feel great about themselves and associate all those feelings with you.'

Listening intently involves way more than listening while planning what you are going to say next. Listening intently demands that you are fully present and fully focused on the person you are listening to. I like to describe it as listening with your heart as well as your head. You strive to still your mind and the constant chatter in your head. All you focus on is the person talking. Let's look at this another way: when last did you feel that someone really listened to you? My guess is that this doesn't happen often. What I do know is that you will remember the person who really listened to you. That person immediately became special because he or she listened intently and made you feel heard.

When People feel Heard, they Feel like they Matter. When People feel Heard, they are more likely to Listen to what You have to Say.

Listening intently performs a very important role in terms of giving you information. By listening intently, you can understand what is important to another person or group. That is vital knowledge that can assist you when you want to connect. It's almost like playing Snakes and Ladders; when you listen intently, you get clues that help you get up the ladder and gain an advantage. If you don't listen intently, you might find yourself slipping down the snake as you didn't spot an obvious clue right in front of you. The clues you get might be as simple as knowing who has been promoted or who is speaking at a conference the next week. Knowing who is connected to whom, not in the sense of who reports to whom but rather who influences which person, can offer other important clues. You might understand who the decision maker really is simply by listening intently. This could save you so much effort!

Very close to listening intently sits observing intently.

I stumbled on this as a young child. My family and I used to play card games, and in those days, we played with actual cards, not cards displayed on a screen. I forget the name of the game we were playing, but I do remember that the jokers in the pack were wild. The game involved each of us holding our cards in our hand. If your turn was next, you had to select a number of cards from someone else. If you selected the joker, you got a huge advantage. By making one simple observation, I was able to win every single game! (I have to confess that I exploited this trick to the extent that the rest of my family refused to play that game with me. I was accused of cheating, and it frustrated everyone that they couldn't figure out how I did it. I also have to confess that I refused to share my secret for a number of years.) I had made one observation that gave me the advantage: I noticed that the white rims around the joker cards were cleaner and brighter than around the other cards. The jokers were not used as often, so they looked newer for longer. That was it, the simple observation that gave me the competitive edge.

When I meet clients for the first time, I observe them closely. Their office is often a good place to learn more about them. What photos are displayed? Are there any awards on the walls? What books or magazines are within view that can give you a point of connection with them? All these details allow you to have a shortcut to connection. If you know what they are passionate about or talented in, you can immediately start talking about those things. This allows you to find common ground, to validate their achievements, and to find shared experiences. You can also observe the level of activity in the environment. You can sense if the pace is frantic, or if people are stressed. Simply commenting on this can also be a point of connection. Listening and observing intently is free, it's uncomplicated, and it works. Use this to connect with others.

As a general rule, I would suggest that comments about achievements, awards and hobbies are unlikely to be interpreted as being too personal. Some people may view comments about their family photos to be an invasion of privacy. If you are in any doubt, keep any observations limited to the work sphere, rather than personal life. Comments about sporting or work-related achievements or books on a shelf are unlikely to make anyone uncomfortable. You want to come across as genuinely interested rather than being nosy.

How to Connect by Listening & Observing Intently:

- Strive to be fully present and focus on the other person.
- Listen with your heart, not only your head. Show genuine interest.
- Comment on what you have heard and keep the focus on the other person
- Observe intently: what personal clues will help you build a connection?
- Observe the level of activity around you.

2. It's Not About You and the Game you are Playing.

Do you remember physical education classes in school? Depending on your love of sports, you probably either loved those lessons (anything beats sitting behind a desk!), or dreaded them. At some point the teacher would pick two people to be the captains of two teams. The captains would then have to take turns choosing their team members. This selection process was often very uncomfortable. It was almost as if your social worth was on display for everyone to see. If you were picked first, you were regarded as more popular, and nobody wanted to be the person who was picked last.

The way I remember it, the selection process went something like this: First, the captains would pick someone who was close to them, like their best friends or relatives. Next, they would pick students who were skilled at the game they were playing. If it was a game of hockey, those good at hockey were selected early, because their skillsets would give the team a competitive advantage. Having them on your team made it more likely your team would win.

After that, captains were likely to choose people who may not be particularly skilled at the game being played, but who were considered good team players. They were fun to be around, and you could rely on them to give it their all and to do whatever they could to help their teams do well.

Those who were selected last were those who, rightly or wrongly, were perceived as not being team players. These people often preferred to operate in isolation. They were not committed to the team, or to the game being played. Sometimes they were hard to get along with and might have been perceived as being difficult.

Your speaking gives the person listening clues as to whether or not they want you on their team. So often we get so wrapped up in our own story or narrative, that we make the mistake of making it all about us. We talk about *our* talents, *our* products, *our* achievements, *our* offering. So why is this a problem? Surely you have to strut your stuff to let people know about you and what you can offer? This is true. However, if you want to be the one who stands out when you speak up, you need to be more perceptive. You need to show how your ideas or products will benefit the person you are speaking to, to demonstrate how you are relevant to them. Your speaking has to be able to connect to them.

When you speak, it is essential that you make clear your ability to add value. What you say has to be meaningful to the person you are speaking to. It has to enrich the conversation.

It is not about you and the game you are playing. It's about your ability to add value to someone else's game.

To demonstrate your ability to add value to someone else's game, you have to have some knowledge of the game they are playing. What is their goal? What are their pain points? What makes them different? What is getting in the way of their success? What makes them successful? For someone to allow you to add value to their game, there has to be a certain level of trust as well as a connection. You need to be perceived as the person they want or need on their team. For that to happen, you need to be someone that is focused on them and not on yourself. Your commitment has to be to make *them* successful. It is not about you. How do you demonstrate that in your speaking?

When I meet clients for the first time, I do my utmost to get to know about their world. They usually come to me when they have a big, important presentation coming up that is way out of their comfort zone. My job as a speech coach is to understand their purpose, their timeline, and what is at stake. I have to go into their world. Often they operate in an industry I have absolutely no knowledge of. On more than one occasion, this industry has been highly technical. This means that I do not understand much of the jargon or technical processes they refer to. I need to be fully present to get a sense of the personality of the speaker. For this reason, I don't offer a one-size-fits-all service. Each client is unique. While the process I take them through to craft their presentation is standard, their outcomes and their presentations are unique. Each is geared to their industry, their unique personality, and their purpose. I would be a lousy speech coach if I tried to fit their presentation into the mould that worked for me.

To add value to their game, you will have to be adaptable and offer something relevant to them, possibly different to what you normally do. You might offer more follow-up, different meeting times, or a different method of communication. All this is designed to build trust, connection and to create a partnership.

To stand out when you speak up and to ensure that you connect, be fully focused on someone else and the game they are playing. It is easier than you think and will deliver results to you.

How to Focus on Others and the Game they are Playing:

- Show genuine interest in the other party: What are they striving for?
- Ask questions that keep the conversation focused on them.
- Discover their successes and their pain points.
- Compliment them on what they have already achieved.
- Relate what you are able to offer to their needs.

3. Connect by Keeping it Personal

One of the easiest ways to make your speaking more personal is to use the name of the person you are speaking to. I make a habit of this when I am anywhere where someone is wearing a name badge. Almost without fail, my taking the time and trouble to greet them by name brings a smile to their face and more attentiveness to their actions. Taking the trouble to thank someone by name also has the power to make someone's day. It costs nothing, is easy to do, and helps you as the customer to connect. I also make it a habit to address support staff by name. Receptionists and PAs play a vital role, and it is good strategy to build a rapport with them in addition to the decision maker.

There is so much value in adding a personal touch to your speaking. Think of the way you would have a conversation with a friend. You are relaxed, confident, and articulate. You share stories of your day and your week easily. It is interesting conversation that is good to listen to. You add in humour very naturally. You can do the same in a business context. But wait: if your speaking is not supposed to be about you, isn't adding a personal touch and sharing a personal story a contradiction?

I will go into more detail on this in another chapter. For now, you need to understand that being personable is another way to connect and to build your reputation. Being relaxed enough to share a personal story makes your unique personality visible. People want to do business with people they like. Allowing someone to get to know you by sharing personal snippets of your life is an effective part of connecting.

I have often shared stories about where I've lived, if there is a relevant point of connection. If I meet someone from Canada, I tell them I had a wonderful year as a Rotary Exchange Student in North Bay, Ontario. If I meet someone with kids and I enquire about their ages, I can relate to the amount of energy it takes to raise kids, having raised three of my own. If the person I am speaking to is passionate about trail running, I can share that I admire them. I love walking, road running, and hiking, but I would be very unsure of myself trail running. In all these examples, I am sharing a brief personal snippet about myself, but my purpose is to find a point of connection with them that can lead to further conversation.

This allows me to get to know them a bit better while allowing both of us to relax, to be ourselves. Make a habit of finding out about people and sharing a little bit about yourself. However, resist the urge to then start telling them about yourself in vivid detail. If you hijack the conversation and make it all about you, you will not connect and will be remembered for the wrong reasons. If that is a habit of yours, you will regularly find people excusing themselves to find someone else to talk to. Remember, a conversation involves give and take. You talk, I listen. Then I talk and you listen. As soon as one of the people involved starts talking for too long, it becomes a monologue, not a conversation. Our tolerance for listening intently to someone who talks too long is very low. Don't be that person.

I remember being invited to lunch by someone who spent the entire meal talking about himself and his plans and achievements. Occasionally that person asked me about what I was doing. No sooner had I started replying, and he said: "That reminds me of when I…." and then promptly hijacked the conversation once again to talk about himself! Be aware of this and resist the temptation to make it all about you. No matter how interesting you are, no one wants to listen to you talking incessantly about yourself.

How to Keep it Personal:

- Make a habit of using names in conversation.
- In meetings, write down the names of people as they are introduced, and strive to address people by name as often as possible.
- Recognise the personal contributions of a person or team.
- Take a genuine interest in the person you are speaking to, and try to find out more about him or her.
- Listen and observe intently to get clues as to what is important to someone else, then use that information as a point of connection.
- Share a brief personal snippet of information about yourself, but only if it is relevant to the person you are speaking to.

4. Connect by Speaking as a Team Player

How do you demonstrate that you are a team player through your speaking? This is an interesting technique. A team player is focused on the game being played and the team playing well. While the game is going on, a good team player leaves the rest of her life on the sidelines. A good team player is fully present and fully focused during game time. A team player who thinks that she is the most important part of the team is not an asset to the team. A team player has one goal: to contribute to the game and help the team win the game. As a team player you understand the rules and abide by them, but that doesn't stop you from being creative or innovative.

Your purpose is to help the team communicate, spot opportunities, and take actions that win the game. A team player will cheer her teammates on, congratulating the ones who perform well. A team player will encourage someone who has made a mistake or is tired. If you are a player who rants and raves that you aren't getting your share of the ball, or who wants the rules changed to suit you, you will not be very popular.

To get a sense of how you play the game, and whether you're playing alone or for your team, ask yourself: How well does your speaking demonstrate that you are a team player? Are you fully focused on the game being played? Does your speaking demonstrate that you are contributing to the team to help them win the game? Do you know the rules? Are you helping your team communicate? Are you helping your team spot opportunities? Does your speaking demonstrate that you are cheering your team members along when they do something right? Does your speaking encourage those team members who are struggling?

If you aren't sure about this, I encourage you to record your speaking during a meeting. Listen to it afterwards and analyse your contribution. It is also important to realise that in order to be a team player, you don't always have to be the nice guy. An important contribution to a team sometimes involves having the difficult conversations. Occasionally you might need to address underperformance. However, you can do so in a manner that respects the person as well as the team. Your speaking needs to reflect that you are there for the good of the team, and that the team is better off due to your contribution.

As you develop the skill of speaking as a team player, you will demonstrate that you are the person other people want on their team. You'll be the person others want to team up with. This is significant! You'll attract opportunity to yourself as teams will seek you out. This also makes it easier for you to find people to work with on a team you are leading. I have had that experience when people have said to me that they will accept the role if I am at the helm. If someone else had asked them, they wouldn't have taken it on. Can you see the impact of this part of speaking and connecting? This is something worth striving for. Keep working on speaking in a way that convinces others that you belong on their team and that they belong on yours.

How to Connect by Speaking as a Team Player:

- Thank individual members for their contributions—on good days and on days that didn't go so well. It takes the contribution of many to make a team.
- Consider who has worked hard to get the team to where they are today. Can you recognise past leaders and team members? What about the people behind the scenes?
- Validate the team leader.
- Celebrate successes, both big and small.
- Honour and thank your supporters.
- Know your strengths and be aware of areas for improvement.

- Remind one another of the game and the goals you are striving for.
- Make sure to have some fun as a team!

5. Connect by Speaking to the Bigger Picture

Our lives are often exceptionally busy and at times chaotic. As we focus on the myriad of tasks at hand, it can be easy to lose sight of the bigger picture. In my experience, losing sight of the bigger purpose often leads to a decline in the levels of motivation. Focusing on the bigger picture can re-energise you. Let me give you a few examples.

Many years ago, I was heading up a fundraising team at my daughter's school. My team and I worked tirelessly for about fifteen months to raise funds for the Matric Dance. It was hard work! We handmade Christmas Crackers and sold them, we hosted comedy evenings, and we sold food and drinks. The dance we were raising funds for was not the dance our own daughters would enjoy. Their turn would come the following year. This year was all about creating a wonderful event for the girls currently in their final year of school. Our daughters were a year younger. When I stepped back and thought about what we were really doing, it was far more than raising funds for a dance. Our purpose was to make memories that lasted a lifetime. This dance was a rite of passage, a milestone that marked their last year at school. The photos would be part of a bank of memories that the girls would look back on for decades to come. Was this a purpose that justified all our hard work? Absolutely! As soon as we focused on the bigger picture, the drudgery and long hours seemed easier to cope with.

At one time in my career, I worked for a company that made basic food items like flour, margarines, and salad dressings. Marketing of commodity items is a challenge. Price plays a huge part in the success of your brand. There are always other brands with a similar offering. However if you speak to the bigger picture as a brand, you go beyond price. In terms of advertising, you address the fact that your brand of flour is reliable. Your brand of flour can be trusted to create beautiful birthday or wedding cakes. Your brand of flour is part of making memories.

Speaking to the bigger picture is an opportunity for you to speak with emotion. Martin Luther King said, 'I have a **dream.**" He didn't say, 'I have a **plan.**" Words like *vision*, *transformation*, and *legacy* carry emotion. Issues that affect the world we live in and our children are emotive.

Craig Valentine, the 1999 World Champion of Public Speaking, taught me a simple way to uncover the benefits of engaging emotion: Use the words 'So that you can…' I am writing this book to help you to speak, connect and succeed, **so that you can** make your voice heard and have more impact every time you speak, **so that you can** get ahead, and **so that you can** make a difference when you speak up.

Our history and heritage are also emotive. Putting your efforts into the context of history and the future helps you speak to the bigger picture. Your vision and the legacy you are building are part of this bigger picture. When I was leading Toastmaster teams, I used to remind the team that it was not about the numbers. In fact, it was about seeing people grow in confidence as they participated in the programme. As they did so, they became more confident. They took this confidence back to their families, their communities and their careers. Our world needs inspirational speakers and leaders, and we worked to make this available to as many people as possible through their Toastmasters membership.

If appropriate, call on people you look up to—perhaps past leaders or present leaders. Speak to their vision or to their legacy.

Take a moment to think about who will benefit from your efforts. How will they benefit? Will some things be easier for them? Or perhaps more efficient? Will they be able to save time? Speak to the benefits far more than to the features of your product or service. We buy benefits, not features. The features are simply there to make the benefit a reality. I go into more detail on this in Chapter 3.

Speaking to the bigger picture usually creates an emotive response as well as an emotional connection with your audience. The bigger picture involves your purpose and your legacy. Remember your final customer and how that person will benefit from your efforts. In meetings, speaking to the bigger picture can often calm tensions and refocus efforts. Speaking to the bigger picture also demonstrates that you get it, that you understand the broader context.

How to Connect by Speaking to the Bigger Picture:

- Think of the ultimate benefit of the work you are doing.
- Use emotive words—'dream' is more emotive than 'plan'.
- The bigger picture can include your history and your heritage.
- The bigger picture can include your vision and the legacy you are building.
- Who inspires you? Why?
- Who benefits from what you are doing? How?

- How will the world be a better place as a result of your efforts?
- To speak to the benefits, complete the phrase: So that you can....

6. Connect by Being Humble, Being Likeable

If your speaking demonstrates that it is not all about you, that you can listen and add value to someone else's game, that you are someone others want on their team, then you come across as humble and likeable. It is possible to be humble while still being ambitious, confident, and driven. A quiet confidence in your own abilities will let people know that you have ambition. Don't fall into the trap of needing to tell everyone how great you are. That is simply annoying.

People do business with people they know, like, and trust. To a large degree, your speaking is the best way to communicate this to others. How else are others going to know that you are someone they like and trust? Consistently demonstrating the qualities we have discussed in this chapter will build and enhance your reputation. At the centre of this lies your authenticity. If you are speaking words and attitudes that you do not believe, this will be immediately evident to someone else. You cannot pay lip service to these attitudes—you have to live them. You need to do so consistently.

How can you speak to demonstrate that you are humble? One of the easiest ways is to avoid needing to be the centre of attention all the time. Keep your focus on the others in the team. Validate their efforts, their talents, and their contributions. Even if you are the leader, you do not need to be the focus of all the attention all of the time. You wouldn't be able to succeed without your team. Make sure your speaking reflects and honours that. Your actions can also demonstrate humility. If you are the leader, don't skip sessions or team building exercises at conferences. Your team needs to see that you are part of the fun and part of the learning. Your absence is often interpreted as arrogance. Speaking as a leader involves speaking to and connecting with those you are leading. Take time to listen to and talk to your team. Being attentive during meetings and conferences speaks volumes about your commitment to the team and to the event, even if you are the guest of honour.

Another powerful way to connect is to speak in a humble way and to share what you have learned from someone else. I saw this in action in my own country. A number of years ago, the Finance Minister in South Africa was Trevor Manuel. He set up a public forum which he called 'Tips for Trevor.' This allowed members of the public, ordinary citizens, to send him tips and advice. Every year when he delivered his budget speech in Parliament, he would quote a tip that he received from a member of the public. He would name that person and read out their suggestion. This was so powerful, because in doing so he came across as accessible, as a leader who both listened and was humble enough to take advice from ordinary citizens.

If you want to be seen as humble and likeable, then have a sense of humour. If you can use self-deprecating humour, even better. Laughing at yourself is a type of humour that is unlikely to offend anyone else. This also demonstrates that you do not take yourself too seriously. Don't think that laughing at yourself will diminish your reputation. On the contrary, it will draw people to you. People who don't take themselves too seriously are fun to be around, and they are likeable.

How to Connect by Being Humble, Being Likeable:

- Let others be the centre of attention.
- Be fully present at events, even if you are the leader.
- Be willing to help and contribute, even if that is not your role.
- Share how others have taught you valuable lessons.
- Have a sense of humour—even at your own expense.

7. Connect by Being Immediately Relevant

If your home is anything like mine, the person who has the TV remote control is the one who has power! We live in a world of incredible choice. We demand instant gratification. If you don't like what you see on the screen in front of you, you simply change channels, again and again if necessary. We don't hesitate to do this—it happens in a nanosecond.

As a speaker, it is important that what you have to say is immediately relevant to the person or group you are speaking to. If not, they will mentally change channels. They may appear to be listening to you, but their minds will be a million miles away. Once their attention has strayed, it is very difficult to get them back. This means that when you speak, you need to be immediately relevant to the person you are speaking to. Before you open your mouth, you need to be aware of who you are speaking to. What do they care about? What do they need to know? How is what you are saying relevant to them? A member of my Mastermind Group, Robyn, put it like this:

Your audience is always thinking:
So what? Make me Care. Do it Fast!

Your challenge is to be immediately relevant to them, not to you. If you achieve this, your audience has a vested interest in listening to what you have to say. The only reason they will listen is if they care about what you are saying. The only way they will care is if it is relevant to them. Always approach your conversations from the point of view and self-interest of the person you are speaking to. This applies to speaking in public as well as to a face-to-face conversation.

Simply by taking a moment before you start a conversation to determine the relevance of what you are saying will change the way you speak. A good way to be relevant is to share a common experience. If you can relate what you are doing or have experienced to their current situation, you can build a connection. Perhaps you have faced and overcome similar challenges in the past. This is a great opportunity to connect and to make your speaking relevant.

To be immediately relevant, it means that you need to get to the point of the conversation right away. Don't waffle at the start of your conversation. So much time is wasted on small talk that no one particularly values. To avoid being abrupt, you can use phrases like 'I know you are very busy, so let me get right to the point.' In my experience, people appreciate the fact that you are concise in your speaking. Being immediately relevant helps me identify why I need to listen to you. Once you have demonstrated that, I want to hear more.

Being immediately relevant ensures that you use your time effectively. Being relevant ensures that you avoid having conversations that lead nowhere. Take a moment before you speak to identify how what you are saying is relevant to your audience. Put yourself in their shoes for a moment. What do they care about? What do they need to hear? Being immediately relevant makes your speaking more powerful.

Questions to ask yourself as you define your relevance: Do you have a common experience that connects you? How can your words or ideas add value to them? If you can become more skilled at being immediately relevant when you speak up, you are more likely to connect.

How to Connect by Being Immediately Relevant when you Speak:

- Listen so that you understand who you are talking to: What are their goals, successes or challenges?
- Let your speaking be immediately relevant to the person you are speaking to by identifying common purposes, experiences and goals.
- How does what you are doing relate to them?
- Can you draw on a common experience that will connect you to them?

Seven Proven Ways to Speak and Connect:

1. Connect by Listening and Observing Intently
Listen and observe, look for clues that will help you connect.

2. It's not about You and the Game You are Playing
Keep your focus on the person you are talking to. How does what you have to say relate to them and their world? This focus will help you speak in a way that is immediately relevant to them. They are far more likely to listen if your speaking is relevant.

3. Connect by Keeping it Personal
Use names, and make your conversation about them. You will get a far better response when your speaking is personal.

4. Connect by Speaking as a Team Player
Your speaking needs to add value to the team. If you make sure it is not all about you, you can demonstrate the value you can add to a team. When you do this well, others will want you on their team.

5. Connect by Speaking to the Bigger Picture
This puts your efforts into context. The bigger picture often speaks to your purpose. Understanding what you are contributing to can be a motivating force for all involved.

6. Connect by Being Humble, Being Likeable
People do business with people they know, like, and trust. Your speaking can demonstrate that. Your speaking can show others that you are a person they want to work with.

7. Connect by Being Immediately Relevant
Being immediately relevant with your speaking is powerful. This helps you get results. When you are immediately relevant, people are far more likely to listen to you. Speaking in a

way that is relevant helps to capture attention. This skill alone can save you time and money as well as build your reputation.

There you have it—7 proven ways to speak and connect. Each of these brings you closer to your goal of connecting with your audience. These have been proven to work for an audience of one as well as an audience of one thousand. Listening is a prerequisite. When you focus on the game that your audience is playing rather than your own game, you are way ahead of most people. By keeping it personal and speaking as a team player, you become more interesting to listen to. Speaking to the bigger picture makes what you say more relevant. Being humble, likeable, and immediately relevant makes you more likely to succeed.

Chapter 3

What is my Purpose? The Power of Intention

Shouldn't it be obvious what your purpose is? A conversation is started to achieve an objective. Or is it? Speaking with purpose is simple and powerful. It doesn't take very long to focus on your purpose—a moment or two is all you need. These few moments will catapult your speaking into another league. Speaking with purpose and intention is not the same as being pushy and insisting on your own agenda. **Speaking with purpose is about knowing where you are heading, setting your compass, and focusing on your goal.** Once again, this is a technique that saves you time. It is a technique that helps you stand out when you speak up.

Often I find myself falling into task mode. I start a conversation and finish it without giving much thought to the purpose upfront. After reading Simon Sinek's book *Start with Why*, I decided to put his theory into action. His premise is that people buy *why* you do something, rather than *how* or *what* you do. Your why—your reason for doing something—speaks to your passion, your purpose, and your intention. When you access passion, you access emotion. Emotion is a powerful connecting tool because when you add purpose and emotion to what you are saying, it is easier for your topic to resonate with someone. If you and I can emotionally identify with an idea, we are more likely to engage with it and take action.

If you truly want to speak, connect and succeed, you need to identify your purpose and intention before the start of any conversation. After reading Simon Sinek's book, I started identifying my why before I wrote any email or made a phone call. The results were quite astounding. I received so much positive feedback about my emails and also my phone calls. I found that more people responded to my emails and replied than ever before. This was the result of starting each email with my why, which often was my purpose. This ensured there was an emotive element that allowed the recipient to connect and engage with me.

You are probably wondering how much time all this will take. You are already super-busy and now I am asking you to take more time before you start speaking. I have to admit to having had similar thoughts! At first it seemed a bit laborious to define my why and my purpose before I started speaking. Very soon it became a habit. Receiving such positive responses further encouraged me to take whatever time I needed. At this point, it takes me very little time to assess my purpose before I send that message, email, or make that phone call. The return on investment for this time and effort makes it worth it.

You are probably familiar with the phrase 'start with the end in mind.' I ask myself what I would like the outcome of the conversation to be. Would I like an appointment with that person, an action to be taken, or agreement on an issue? Then I further define exactly what that outcome would look like. This focus allows me to be more intentional about my speaking. This avoids the situation where a conversation has ended and I suddenly realise that I forgot to mention one important item. In other words, by spending a little bit of time in preparation, I am more likely to be efficient and to achieve my goals. I have also found that people appreciate this purpose and intention. Time is precious to all of us. By going into a conversation or meeting with purpose and intention, I honour everyone's time. Meetings can be so pointless and often achieve nothing. You can change that by being purposeful and intentional when you speak.

Defining your purpose leads to clarity. Clarity of purpose and intention leads to positive results. This process certainly doesn't guarantee that you will always have things going your way, and you may not always achieve your purpose. But by being intentional, you guarantee that your speaking supports your purpose. You make it easier for others to understand you and what you want to achieve.

This process is especially important when you need to have a conversation that is uncomfortable or difficult on some level. By spending a bit of time defining your purpose, you will find it easier to address any thorny issues during your conversation. The preparation ahead of time allows you to engage purposefully with the issue at hand. This means that during the conversation, you are replying in a more considered way. With purpose and intention clearly defined, you are more likely to truly respond rather than merely react.

I have applied this technique on the most important of conversations—those with my teenage children. I find that when I am intentional and speak with purpose, I can address difficult issues more calmly. It is easier to stay on topic and to avoid responding emotionally when your buttons are being pushed. I am now more likely to have a positive outcome to the difficult discussions compared to when I didn't start the conversation with purpose.

Defining your purpose is also an opportunity to see how this conversation fits into the bigger picture. How important is this person to you and what you are doing? Is it worth your time to foster a deeper relationship with this person? What would be the benefits of doing so? Can you, or do you need to, position yourself as an asset to this person or this team? What can you bring to the team that they would find useful? How can you help them overcome their challenges? How can you add value to the game they are playing? Being aware of the answers to these questions ahead of your conversation will make your speaking more purposeful and effective.

Another way to define your purpose is to ask yourself what you want the other person to think, feel or do differently as a result of hearing you speak. How would they benefit from hearing your ideas? What can they avoid if they follow your suggestions? What is the cost of inaction to them?

Being purposeful and intentional about your conversations can deliver spectacular results. Don't wing it, even if you are naturally confident. Spend a bit of time preparing for the conversation by defining what you could gain and what you could lose. Be focused and purposeful. This is a process that makes your speaking more efficient and helps your speaking deliver the results you are looking for.

Speak, Connect and Succeed
Speak with Purpose Process
To ensure you get results with Every Call,
Every Conversation, Every Email

What is the purpose of this call, conversation, email, or message?
What do you want to achieve as a result of this conversation?

What is at stake?
What could you gain if this goes well? What could you lose? What happens if nothing changes?

If I only had ten words to use, what would those ten words be?
Be concise. Get to the point. Don't waffle. State your intention.

How will my audience benefit from what I have to say?
Don't assume they will get this. State the benefits to those involved. Think of the issue from their viewpoint.

What could my audience avoid if they took action?
Is there a potential problem that could be avoided? What is the cost of inaction?

What is my call to action?
What comes next? Say this clearly. Establish if you have agreement, and if not, what needs to be clarified? Do you need to get other people on board?

What needs to happen next? Who will take the next step? By when? When will I follow up?
Don't allow the ball to be dropped and for no action to be taken. It must be clear who is taking the next step, by when. When will you have a follow-up conversation?

How can I end off on a positive note?

This is important, especially if this was a difficult conversation. Give thanks for the contributions and acknowledge if it was a challenging conversation. Refer back to the bigger picture and purpose.

What or who can I validate?

Every contribution is valuable, even if it is an opposing point of view. There is great power in making people feel heard.

Speaking with purpose is simple and powerful. It doesn't take very long to focus on your purpose—a moment or two is all you need. These few moments will catapult your speaking into another league. Speaking with purpose and intention is not the same as being pushy and insisting on your own agenda.

Speaking with purpose is about knowing where you are heading, setting your compass, and focusing on your goal.

Once again, this is a technique that not only saves you time but also helps you build your reputation every time you speak.

Chapter 4

What is my Message and Why do I Need One?

This chapter forms the foundation of the process I take each of my clients through. Finding your message is powerful. Your message helps you deliver on your purpose, and it helps you focus your attention and your audience's on your why.

**Information alone doesn't connect;
It's your message that has the power
to make your information come alive.**

Your message gives your audience a vested interest in listening carefully to what you have to say, and your message has a far higher chance of being remembered than your information.

I can confidently share that this is the one technique that has had the greatest impact on my speaking and my ability to connect with my audience. Learning about having a message when I speak has transformed my speaking, and learning the process of finding my message has saved me an inordinate amount of time.

I used to jump in and start preparing a presentation without much thought. I would start designing PowerPoint slides with great enthusiasm, spending time choosing the perfect background, theme, and design. By the time I got to the fifth slide, I would often discover I had no idea where this presentation was going. At this point, I might be two or three hours into the process before realizing I was wasting time and energy designing slides for a presentation that I hadn't thought through. What a waste of time! If this sounds familiar to you, this chapter will help you save yourself hours and hours of time!

Speaking without a message is similar to speaking without a purpose. You could talk for days and not get through to your audience. Every conversation has a purpose, commonly to inform, to persuade, or to entertain. Unless you are speaking to yourself and are happy to listen to your own ramblings, you're likely to have a purpose for speaking to begin with. But even when you have a purpose, you still need to have a message. **Speaking without a message will make it harder to connect with your audience.** A message makes adding emotion to your speaking easier, and emotion connects.

The difference between delivering a message and delivering only information is vast. Many speakers fall into the trap of giving the audience an information dump. They cram years of knowledge into a short presentation. Perhaps they believe the myth that the more information you can squeeze into a presentation, the higher your credibility. Nothing could be further from the truth. If you are dumping information onto your audience, you run the risk of losing not only your audience, but any opportunity you might have gained through that presentation. On top of that, you can damage your reputation. I often hear that speakers at international conventions are dreadfully boring. They are usually asked to speak based on their credentials, not their ability to communicate. But what a lost opportunity for them if they fail to connect with their audience and communicate their message.

Information is made up of facts and data, and it dwells in the brain and the head. Of course, facts and data can be vital to making or proving a point, but if you're not careful they can also get in the way of delivering a message. Often, facts and data aren't emotive in any way, and it can be difficult for an audience to relate to them. Mostly, facts aren't personal, so there's no personal connection for the audience. Let's face it—facts alone can be deadly boring to listen to.

By contrast, a message is emotive, and it comes from the heart. There's a personal element, usually a strong belief or passion, lying behind a message. Messages, almost by defini-tion, have a purpose.

Messages illuminate how facts and data are relevant to the audience, making numbers and technicalities come alive!

Messages are designed to elicit a response or a reaction. The best messages are short, memorable, and repeatable. This is a concept I was first introduced to by Craig Valentine, the co-author of *World Class Speaking in Action*. He refers to this as a foundational phrase. Think T-shirt: the kinds of slogans companies print onto shirts are short, sometimes humorous, and usually memorable. Often they arouse curiosity about a topic or an issue.

I first came across the power of having a message when I was heading up a team a number of years ago. We held a training event, and it was my first opportunity to address my extended team. I was thinking about what to say. I knew that they all expected me to challenge them to do well that year and to achieve results. That was predictable. However, I wanted to deliver my message in a way they would remember, a way that might elevate my speaking beyond what they were already expecting to hear.

One afternoon, I went to a shopping centre near my home. I parked my car and made my way down to the shopping area. As I came down the escalator, something caught my eye. At the bottom of the escalator, I saw the Levi Jeans store, with a big poster hanging in the window, showing four people in a white convertible driving through a forested area.

The people in the car were young, beautiful, and of course, happened to be wearing Levi Jeans clothing. The driver was smiling with one hand on the steering wheel and the other resting on the side of his door. The guy in the passenger seat was kneeling on the seat, facing backwards. He was talking, smiling, and gesturing to the two girls in the back. I had no idea what he was saying, but it was evident that these four people were having the time of their lives. The tagline at the bottom of the poster read: 'I refuse to sit at home and gather dust.'

As I thought about this, I knew that this was the message I had been looking for. When individuals, teams, or companies take no action, they gather dust. If you continue to do what you have always done, without innovating, you are in danger of gathering dust. Items and people that gather dust lose their appeal. Often we avoid contact with dusty objects. We lose sight of their value. If it gets really bad, we discard the item. This phrase became my message for my presentation. I knew it resonated with my audience as they quoted those words back to me often during that year. When your words are quoted back to you long after you have said them, your message has gotten through. It was short, memorable, and repeatable. Most importantly, it resonated with my audience.

So how do you go about defining your message? This is a process I take all my clients through, irrespective of their topic. I challenge them to distill their entire presentation into ten words or less. Given the vast amount of knowledge you might have on a subject, this is no easy task, but it ensures that you have absolute clarity of thought on your presentation. If you have ever heard a speaker ramble on and on, it is usually because he or she didn't have a clear distilled concept for the presentation. If you aren't crystal clear on your topic, there is virtually no chance that your audience will be clear either. Remember that most of your audience won't be very familiar with your topic. Your audience only gets to hear your presentation once. By contrast, you may have studied, lived, and breathed your topic for years. Perhaps it makes perfect sense to you, but it isn't likely to be so obvious to your audience.

Here is a process to help you define your message:

Challenge yourself to write down twenty different ten-word statements about your presentation. At this point, don't think too much—just do a brain dump. As you do this, you will find that you keep refining the wording, and soon enough, one or two of those phrases will jump out at you as being the best ones.

Don't be afraid to have some fun with this. Add a bit of humour or borrow from famous advertising taglines and film titles. Test the slogan with friends or family. Once you have this slogan defined, weave it into your presentation. Use it in your title if appropriate. Make sure you use it at the beginning of your presentation. Try to repeat it a few times, and then end with it.

The statistics about how long people remember what you have said after you finish speaking are depressing. You and your words are soon forgotten. But having a message repeated a few times makes it easier for people to remember both you and your topic. By creating a powerful message, you ensure that you are remembered for all the right reasons—much preferable to being remembered for being boring and uninspiring!

If you are like me, you are busy almost all the time. Going through this process to identify and define your message will save you time, lots of time. When your message is clear, it becomes easy to see what has to stay in your presentation and what has to be removed. Your message helps you deliver on your purpose. When your message is clearly defined, it is easier to stay focused and concise. Think about what you appreciate about speakers who are concise and to the point. They don't waste your time, and you have all the information you need to take the next step. Make sure you are the speaker who does this for your audience. And make sure you aren't the speaker who drones on and on and on.

Speak, Connect and Succeed
How to Find your Message
And Make your Information come Alive

If you only had ten words to say, what would those ten words be?

Write down as many versions of ten word statements as you can. Keep playing with them until you come up with one that is short, memorable, and repeatable. Would you put this on a T-shirt? This step ensures that you have absolute clarity of thought. If you aren't crystal clear, there is no chance your audience will be either.

What is the most important concept you want to communicate?

This is often your why. Of everything you want to say, what is the most important?

How will your audience benefit from what you have to say?

Are you solving a problem? Are you creating a possibility? How will their lives improve if they apply your ideas?

What is it that you want them to think, feel, or do differently?

Be specific. Connect the dots for them and never assume they will see everything the way you do. Your audience only gets to hear your presentation once, so you need to be clear and memorable.

Why does this matter so much to you?

You could have chosen many topics, so why this one? When did this become important to you? Can you think of the moment it did? What impact has this discovery had on your life? When your audience knows why you care, they find it easier to relate to you and what you are saying.

When you consistently take the time to define your message, you will not only save time, but your speaking will be much more powerful. You will have far more clarity in your speaking. This will make it easier for your audience to understand, follow, and remember you. Your message will help your information come alive.

Best of all, you will find that the time you need to prepare your speech or presentation will decrease significantly. As I have become more skilled in using this method, I can also sense whether or not my message has what it takes to resonate with an audience. Once I reach that point, I am so much more confident going into that presentation.

I apply this same process when I prepare for phone calls, emails, messages, and meetings. Before I make a call or send a message, I take a moment to prepare. I try to identify and clarify my message. As a result, my speaking is far more purposeful and effective. Try this—it will transform the outcome of your conversations, your meetings and your communication. In the next chapter, I will show you how to inspire others when you speak up. This is one of my favourite techniques. Regardless of what you do for a living or are passionate about, the ability to inspire people when you speak up is a skill you want to be able to call on. Your team, your family, and your community will benefit when you can speak to inspire.

Chapter 5

How do I Speak to Inspire?
What Happens when I Do?

Why is it useful to inspire others when you speak? Simply put, it is easier to achieve your purpose when you can inspire others to take action or to buy into your ideas. Think of people you have heard speak—the more inspiring they are, the more you like to listen to them. The more inspiring they are, the more likely you are to take action.

Almost by definition, **speaking in an inspiring manner demands that you add emotion to your presentation.** Martin Luther King, in his famous speech, didn't say: I have a *'plan'*. No—he deliberately used the word *'dream'*. This is a word that is far more emotive than *'plan'*. Inspirational speakers speak of hopes and dreams and aspirations. They speak about things common to us, things we care about. Often they refer to universal experiences or events that are familiar and important to all of us. Their speaking promises a future where experiences have the potential to turn from negative to positive. Often they speak about many people uniting as one, rather than being divided. The language they use is emotive, yet simple to understand.

Inspirational speaking validates effort and recognises struggles. This kind of speaking honors not only individuals' contributions, but their worth. When you speak inspirationally, you show passion, and you let me know what you care deeply about. Inspirational speaking also expresses belief in what is yet to come. Consider the popular phrase 'I know we can…' Inspirational speaking speaks to potential, to possibility, to hope. You speak about overcoming fear and obstacles and about creating possibilities. Inspirational speaking often includes humour, added personal stories that make the presentation more entertaining and easier to relate to.

When I look back at my corporate career, not many leaders with a real talent for inspiring their teams come to mind. Too often, they emphasised the mundane and the boring stuff. Don't get me wrong—every organisation absolutely needs to pay attention to the everyday. That's non-negotiable, since small, routine tasks are building blocks for success. However, as a leader or team member, you have the opportunity to address those matters in an inspiring way. If you can connect with and inspire your team, you will get buy-in for even the mundane. Speaking to inspire requires that you put things in perspective. When what you are doing serves a higher purpose, one that is meaningful to you and your team, you will all be motivated and inspired to deliver.

Our whole department was summoned into the boardroom mid-afternoon. This didn't happen very often, so we knew something was up. The head of our department, a director of the company, called us together to highlight a few things that were bothering him. Among this list was the fact that people were arriving at work late. He spoke in a mild-mannered way, but there was not an iota of inspiration in what he said. I remember leaving that meeting feeling irritated rather than inspired. We had been spoken to like school children. There was no interaction or discussion, and I didn't feel like I was part of a team. What a missed opportunity!

Knowing what I know now, if I had been the leader, I would have approached that meeting as an opportunity to inspire my team. Teams thrive on validation and recognition. I would have recognized the achievements of our team—I would have found something to celebrate and would have highlighted our goals and aspirations as a team, to remind all of us about the bigger picture.

Within that context, I would have addressed the late-coming and challenged the team to improve. How would we benefit if we all arrived on time? What was the impact on the team when that didn't happen? I would have asked for feedback. There is so much power when people hear from their peers how their behavior affects them. I would have added some humour and ended on a positive note. I would have thanked them for their contributions to the team and told them that I was proud to be their leader. I would have spoken with the clear goal that they left inspired rather than irritated.

In retrospect, it's easy for me to see in that meeting an opportunity our leader didn't notice at the time: an opportunity to inspire. **Consider that every time you speak, you have an opportunity to inspire.** It's helpful to me to think in terms of what I call the *Speaking to Inspire Palette*. As the name implies, this is a collection of facets of inspiration that you can incorporate to add an inspirational element to your speaking. You don't have to use all of them all of the time. Instead, focus only on those that are appropriate and that work for you. Remember that at all times what you say has to be authentic. Don't for a moment think that you can tick all the boxes and still be speaking to inspire. If you don't believe something, don't say it.

As human beings, we all experience self-doubt. It seems that we continually question our own abilities. What fascinates me is that we somehow believe and accept someone else's opinion far more easily than we believe our own. You might consider yourself to be a talented designer or auditor, and yet, many times, you probably doubt yourself. Then along comes a colleague who sings your praises, and it's *their* words of validation that inspire you, get you to take the next step, and make you believe what you are capable of. *Your* words to someone else have that same power—far beyond what you've ever imagined. Seek every opportunity to use your words to inspire another. Think of inspirational speaking as something that has to be done regularly and repeatedly. Just like flowers need to be watered to grow, so people need to be inspired and validated regularly to be at their best.

Personal words of encouragement and validation are far more prized than trophies, certificates, and titles. Occasionally, I have been lucky enough to receive a message from people who have written to me to comment on how I have inspired them. These notes are treasures that I keep in a special file. The people who wrote them may have forgotten they did so. For me, these notes live on in perpetuity—I even refer to them from time to time, and their power comes alive every time I read them. Your words of encouragement and thanks have the potential to inspire others.

Your words are equally powerful. Think back on someone who encouraged and inspired you. I bet you can remember their words as well as how those words made you feel. By speaking with purpose, drawing from the Speaking to Inspire Palette, you have the potential to connect with and impact the lives of many people with your words. I don't know about you, but that is a possibility I want to be part of!

One of the aspects of speaking to inspire is adding your personal story into the mix. Tell someone how their actions or words have impacted you. It is a huge compliment to someone when you remember their words and then take it further and act on them. The fact that you then take the additional trouble to give them that positive feedback will be greatly appreciated. If you want to be the person to connect and to stand out when you speak up, you have to add value to the team and the game they are playing. Being a team member who can inspire and validate others makes you a huge asset to the team. If you have an abundance of talent and knowledge but upset everyone when you interact with them, you won't be able to inspire.

A few years ago, I had the privilege of running an *Inspirational Leadership* workshop in Harare, Zimbabwe. My approach to any training I do is to closely monitor the mood of the delegates as the day progresses. I had quite a bit of material I wanted to cover. However, I came to the realization that this team needed to speak to and hear from one another. About thirty people were attending, and most seemed to know one another and had worked together.

I discarded my planned agenda and asked them to choose another person in the room and tell them how they had been inspirational. To add a bit of fun, I had some colourful flower garlands and gave the delegates the opportunity to place a garland, or two, or three on someone when they validated them. This process was so inspiring for all involved. One by one, the delegates got to hear from others how their efforts had been inspirational—even for those tasks they thought no-one even noticed. Some blushed as they heard how they had inspired another, others looked sheepish receiving an unexpected compliment. The energy in the room shifted. There was an outpouring of appreciation that left each one of us humbled and feeling grateful. The result was that this team of people had connected in a unique way. Not only had they received validation, they had been afforded the opportunity to validate one another. The room was filled with smiling faces, confident attitudes and colourful garlands. This team had bonded in a unique and memorable way.

Validation is a powerful leadership tool. Having the space and the opportunity to validate one another helps to build team spirit. Seeing the range of behaviours that others considered inspirational was fascinating. Some were validated for demanding excellence, others for always being at meetings. Some were validated for challenging the status quo, others for sharing an encouraging word. Consistently meeting deadlines on time was an inspiration for some. Ending meetings on time was considered to be inspirational by others. The success of this workshop lay in the opportunity to give and receive validation. If your team lacks inspiration, start finding opportunities to validate. Make this a habit—it will stand you in good stead and will help you speak, connect and succeed.

Speak, Connect and Succeed Inspiration Palette

Validation
Validate the person or team by speaking about what they have already achieved. What are they known for?

Context
How does what they are doing fit into the bigger picture? What contribution are they making?

Keep it Personal
Use their name. Refer to where they are based. Speak to what makes them unique.

Recognition of Contribution
Speak to what they have contributed. Be specific and quote examples.

Charismatic Listening
Be fully present. Listen attentively. Give them the space to share and be fully heard. Many people don't get much opportunity to share their success story.

Impact
Speak to the impact that their specific contribution has on the whole, whether in the form of tasks completed, attitude demonstrated, tenacity, or something else.

Future Vision
Speak to where you see this person or team going in the future. What could they achieve? What impact could they have?

Gratitude
Speak to how you feel working with this person or team. Personally thank them for what they do. How have they impacted you? How have they inspired you?

Speaking to inspire is a way to be sure your words resonate with your audience. As you have seen, inspiration and validation are closely linked. Inspiration not only demands an emotive element, but inspiration thrives on emotion. Inspiration is powerful, and an inspired audience is far more likely to allow your words to influence a change in their behaviour.

To put it really simply, if you can inspire, your speaking has incredible impact on your audience. You can influence tremendous change through inspiration. Always remember that inspirational speaking has a place in every conversation you have, every message you send, and every post you put on social media. It is not confined to platform speaking

Chapter 6

How do I Speak to Persuade?

We speak to persuade one another on a daily basis. On any given day, I might try to persuade one of my kids to cook dinner or my husband to watch a movie I chose. You could try and persuade someone to do it your way, to join you for coffee, or to be on your task team. Persuasion is innate to us. When we speak or give presentations, we especially need to be able to weave in persuasive techniques. When we get this right, we have a much higher chance of getting someone to buy into our vision or adopt our way of thinking. You may not be a salesperson, but chances are that you need to be persuasive on a daily basis.

What happens when we aren't able to persuade others? Often it means that our ideas never see the light of day. It can mean that your idea or approach is overlooked, even if it is the best option available. If you are unable to persuade others, your career prospects may be quite limited. You will find yourself going along with the ideas of others, even if those ideas are inferior to yours.

What if I could show you how to be persuasive without being bossy or overbearing? What if you had a process that you could follow as a guide? What would that mean to you?

One of the biggest compliments I received was in the form of a humorous story as told by a colleague of mine, Lazola. He was part of an extended team I led. I would call Lazola from time to time to check in with him and see how he was doing. Those phone calls were also purposeful, as I would try to motivate him to take a certain course of action to get the results we were looking for.

Sometime later, Lazola told a group of us a story. He shared with us that when he saw my name come up on his phone, he would want to answer, but often he would let it ring a little bit longer. The reason? Lazola had come to know that I could be very persuasive. He described it as knowing that he would agree to whatever I suggested! That was confirmation that it pays to be able to persuade when leading a team.

If you want to hone your persuasive skills, pay careful attention to this chapter. **Being persuasive is a key part of connecting, increasing your influence and building your reputation,** and if you don't work on it, many opportunities may pass you by.

I learned so much about persuasive techniques by having to follow an administrative process. I had to learn these skills quickly when I started my career in marketing management working for a big multinational company as a brand manager. When we wanted to launch a product or make any changes to a product, we had to complete an Authorisation to Proceed form. This innocuous-looking document detailed all the changes we were proposing. To get approval for these changes, I had to personally meet with and persuade fourteen heads of department that my idea was a good one. This took much effort and time, and I learned so much in the process, including that if I wasn't able to connect and persuade, I wouldn't be able to make progress.

Each of these heads of department looked at my proposal from a different viewpoint. I had to get approval from the technical department, the legal department, the finance department, and many more. I was a relatively junior member of staff, yet often I would have to persuade directors of the company and senior managers. I couldn't go into those meetings without having done my research. My pre-work consisted of meetings and consultations with a variety of people. I had to answer all their queries and concerns in a positive way before someone would sign my form. It wasn't ever a given that the authorities would all agree. I had heard stories of one director who refused to sign off on one form despite the fact that thirteen other departments had already approved it.

This rigorous process taught me to approach the issue from the point of view of the person whose approval I needed. What were their concerns? What did they know that I needed to be informed or aware of? Each one of these people were experts in their field. I had very limited knowledge of their department. There were production issues that I needed to know about and financial considerations that were key to the decision-making process. Only when I listened attentively and engaged these departments was I able to make progress.

My proposal needed to demonstrate that I understood the issue from their point of view. In this instance, my persuasive skills only came into play after much work and attention to detail. I learned so much from this process. Much of what I am sharing with you in this chapter was learned during that time in my career.

Then, Now, and How

One of the simplest persuasive techniques I have come across comes from Craig Valentine. He refers to this as his 'Then, Now, and How' technique.

Let's break down the steps and consider them individually.

THEN—Take a historical approach, and begin by describing an issue as it was before your solution came along. What worked or didn't work? How long did it take? What were the challenges? What were the pain points? Where did the frustrations lie?

NOW—Describe the transformation following the implementation of your idea. What's working well? How long did it take to work? What is easier or better? What is possible for you now that was not possible before? How do you feel about this?

HOW—What led to the change? What action did you take that made this change a reality? How can your audience take advantage of this? How will they benefit? What is the exact next step you want them to take?

It goes without saying that in order to be persuasive, you need to know your purpose. What is the outcome you are looking for? What needs to change? Why?

Part of the persuasive process is to remove any possible fears that someone else might have about making a change. You need to reassure them that the change is worthwhile. Keep on stating your message. In Chapter 4 you learned how to clearly define your message. Be sure to complete that process before working on being persuasive.

Persuasion also involves listening. Speaking for myself, I am unlikely to be persuaded by someone who won't listen to my input or point of view. It's important to validate the opinions of others, even if they are contrary to yours. One of my mentors, Erich, was very skilled at this. When he runs workshops, he is careful to positively acknowledge every single contribution—even those that may not be very useful. He thanks the person for their contribution and makes them feel heard. That immediately creates a positive mindset that can be used to take the discussion further.

Another technique Erich introduced me to was that of saying 'Yes...and' rather than 'Yes...but'. Your objective at this point is to keep engaging people on the issue. The worst thing that can happen is that you get someone's back up and find the conversation shut down. When that happens you aren't likely to be able to be persuasive at all.

A persuasive speaker speaks to the potential benefits for their audience. If there are multiple parties involved, discuss the benefit to each of them. How would the change benefit the customer? How about the admin staff? What impact will this change have on the production process? What about the financial impact? The more well-considered and well-thought-out your argument is, the higher your chance of being persuasive. At all times, you have to state *what happens next*. What specific action do you want the person to take?

Keep talking about the bigger picture. Can you refer to universal experiences, hopes, or dreams? What fundamental, shared beliefs come into play?

Another persuasive technique is to proactively raise any objections the listener might have. Craig Valentine uses this technique when he says: 'I know what you are thinking...' This technique works well as it addresses potential objections. It also demonstrates that you are in touch with how your listener views the world. It reassures them that you understand and value their viewpoint.

I recently shared this technique with a client of mine. She was going into a strategic planning session, informing a leadership team about trends in the market. Her research had shown her what the company needed to do next. I encouraged her to proactively state that some parts of the discussion would possibly make the team feel uncomfortable. They were considering venturing into new territory. By addressing this issue ahead of time and encouraging the team to not shut down, the debate, although rigorous, was productive.

Always remember that persuasion is not always an event—it is mostly a process. This persuasive process takes time. You might have to have this persuasive conversation many times before you succeed. Your challenge is to make the persuasive points as often as appropriate. Please, please, please don't become a nag. That is very off-putting and won't do your reputation any favours!

Speak, Connect and Succeed Persuasive Process

What do I want to achieve?
State it simply and clearly.

Who will benefit?
There may be more than one person who will benefit.

How?
Be specific. How will their circumstances or prospects improve?

What is my ten-word message on this topic?
Having your ten-word statement defined makes sure that you have clarity of thought.

What are the current issues? Problems? Challenges? Frustrations?
This addresses what is not working. It helps to spend time exploring the pain, reminding people how bad things are.

What needs to change?
What changes are needed? Do they represent a change in attitude or process? How big or small a change are we considering?

What would the benefit be?
Be specific. What would be easier, more efficient or benefit more people?

What potential objections will be raised?
Do your homework. See the issue from the other viewpoint. Anticipate your listener's concerns.

What universal experiences or beliefs can you tap into?
Connect with your audience by demonstrating an understanding of their motivations and concerns.

What emotions are present?
Acknowledge the range of emotions present—they are powerful.

How can you demonstrate that you are listening?
What have you heard? What have you understood?

Remember to validate all responses.

The ability to persuade is an essential technique in your daily life. Once you become aware of how often your conversations are already persuasive, you will see multiple opportunities to hone this skill. When a person tries to sell me their point of view or a service, I am now very aware of the techniques they are using. I am in a better position to analyse their approach to ensure that I agree with their point of view. If not, I can very easily determine the reasons why. A knowledge of persuasive techniques makes you not only better at selling your own ideas, but it makes you a more savvy customer, too.

Chapter 7

The Power of Keeping it Personal

It's not always easy to be the one to stand out. We are bombarded with messages and links crammed with information on a daily basis. So much information competes for our headspace. We live in a world of abundant choice, and still, whatever we do, we are usually one of many doing the same thing. One of the most powerful ways to get someone's attention and to connect is to keep your speaking personal.

At a very young age, people learn to respond to their names. It is hard to ignore someone when they call you by name. (Of course the opposite happens when your name is overused, which can be interpreted as nagging.) Young children insist on personal attention and often go to great lengths to get it. With kids, the best way to respond is to make direct eye contact with them, at their eye level, and to simply listen. Somehow we forget that this tactic works for adults, too.

The problem is that our world is often very impersonal. We are more connected digitally than ever before. However, in my opinion, human connection still trumps digital connection. Somehow when someone uses your name in the right way, you feel more cared for, and you're more likely to respond positively. You are highly likely to remember the person using your name. If that person has a real conversation with you, rather than a digital one, it has more impact on you.

I have met many people who are very hesitant to pick up a phone and have a conversation. They prefer the safety and distance of digital messaging. The assumption is that most people are in constant contact via their phone. This may be true. However, actually speaking to someone on the phone can be far more effective than endless digital messages. If you are uncomfortable making phone calls or speaking in person, make a commitment to do so regularly—even if you are initially uncomfortable.

When everyone else is sending digital messages, you stand out when you choose to make a phone call. Meeting in person trumps a phone call. When you are sitting face-to-face having a conversation, you have a much better sense of how the other person is reacting to what you have to say. Your responses can be moderated easily as the conversation flows. This is not very easy to do when you are communicating digitally. A face-to-face conversation is a much richer experience (4D), a phone call a more muted experience (2D), and a digital conversation a very restricted experience (1D).

Simply by adding more personal touches to your speaking, you can ensure that you connect when you speak.

Use Names as Often as Possible

For the next few days, take every opportunity you can find to address someone by name. When you are out shopping or in a restaurant, look for someone wearing a name badge and address that person using their name. My experience is that when I address someone by their name, the first thing that happens is that he or she makes eye contact with me. Shortly thereafter, a smile appears. I use those moments of connection to comment or enquire about how their day is going. If it is evident that the restaurant or store is very busy, I comment on how they are coping. In many ways, this is a form of validation—you are simply recognising them and the effort they are putting into their job. People respond very positively to this and appreciate the fact that you not only are speaking to them personally, but that you are speaking in a positive way.

At work, make a habit of addressing people by name, especially support staff. Go out of your way to get to know people you work with, even those in different departments. If you want to stand out when you speak up, you need to connect with people regularly. The more you practice, the more skilled you become.

Those people who have mastered the art of remembering names are way ahead of everyone else. I experienced the effect of this when I attended my 25th school reunion. My high school maths teacher, Pam Ellis, later became the principal of the school. I had not seen her in 25 years, but she took one look at me, paused, and then addressed me by name! I was blown away. She had a real talent for remembering names. Of course, I haven't forgotten hers either. If you master this skill, you become unforgettable.

I try to work on this skill constantly. If I am in a meeting, I write down the names of all the people there, as a tactic to help me remember. It is wonderful as a trainer to be able to call on people by name. When running a workshop, I will insist that there are name cards in front of each person to make it easier for me to learn names and to address people by their name.

I was very impressed recently when I went into the offices of a retail clothing company with a head office in Cape Town. They have a policy that every staff member wears a name badge every day. It is a pleasure being able to go there and easily call people by their name. Having this practice in an office environment will inevitably lead to a more personable interaction among people. As a visitor, it was an enormous help as it became easy to address people by name and keep my speaking personal.

On the practical side, when you create name badges, please make sure that they are legible. Having a name badge with a name printed in small font is not helpful at all. Print the names in bold, in a large font that is easy to read. My personal preference is for name badges with my first name in bold. In a more formal setting, both the first name and the surname need to be in large font, printed in bold. Lanyards with name tags that are only visible at waist level are also annoying. My preferred option are name badges that are worn on lapels, just below shoulder level.

Send Personalised Messages

A few years ago, I discovered that keeping it personal was a leadership tool. I was leading an extended team. A friend of mine volunteered to assist me. She asked me what I wanted to be known for during my term of office. I responded that it was important for me to have personal contact with the members of the organisation. Together we came up with a plan to do this.

My friend, Merryl, helped me devise a series of personal emails. In Toastmasters, members deliver speeches according to set criteria as they work through the programme. Each speech is a challenge. I wrote a series of emails—each focusing on a different speech. In total, I must have created about fifteen different emails. Merryl and I devised a system to send a personalised email from me to the speaker, relevant to the project they were completing. This took a great deal of work, and I will forever be grateful to Merryl for helping me create a system to do this. The effect was profound—I have had people come up to me years later and thank me for sending them a personal email when they were about to deliver their third speech. Having a leader take a personal interest in you makes an impact. If you are a leader, be sure to connect on a personal level with your team. This is sure to help you connect and succeed.

The Power of Personal Calls

I also took on the challenge to call not only the leaders of my team but also the key people who reported to those leaders. There was a chain of command in place—one that worked well depending on who was in which role. My calling people who did not report to me was unusual, since there were about two to three layers of leadership between me and them. But I wanted to establish a relationship with them upfront—long before I might call them when we were working towards specific goals and deadlines.

The primary purpose of these calls was to connect. I would do a great deal of listening to understand their challenges. I would make a point of validating their efforts. On these calls, I would refer to the leaders in the team in a positive way. My call was always in support of the team. I would follow up the call with a personal email, copying the other leaders involved. That way, everyone was aware of my call and of my support for the team. This strategy took time and energy, but the investment delivered a return. The result was a team of motivated and inspired leaders who were grateful for support expressed in a personal phone call.

In terms of sending emails or messages, the more personal you make them, the higher your response rate. When I was encouraging teams to achieve goals, I would take a screenshot of their particular results to date. That would be in the body of the email. That screenshot gave details that allowed me to commend them on what they had already achieved. It also allowed me to draw their attention to the fact that they were close to achieving certain targets. I always expressed confidence that they knew what to do and had what it took to do it. I made them aware that they were part of a bigger team. We were working towards goals that would leave a legacy. I was proud to have them on my team. Once again, this strategy took time and effort, but here too, the positive response and the results we achieved made clear that the effort was well worth it. As you can see from these examples, keeping it personal includes validating and inspiring people. It is difficult to inspire someone if you don't keep it personal.

A friend also demonstrated to me the power of keeping it personal. At the time we didn't know one another well. We had an appointment set up, but Mandy needed to postpone our meeting. She sent me an email informing me of the change, but what I found extraordinary was that she acknowledged the impact of that change on me. She made clear that she understood my schedule might be impacted and I would probably be disappointed. The fact that she had thought about this from my point of view and had taken the trouble to articulate this to me made her stand out. I have adopted this practice whenever I find myself in a similar situation.

What I learned from Hallmark Cards

If you are like me, you appreciate being able to walk into a shop and buy a special-occasion card. I often purchase Hallmark cards. They are great, because you are bound to find one with a message that can be personalised and given to someone for almost any occasion.

This is wonderful for special occasions, but it isn't great for your speaking. I have often heard people giving very general, bland speeches that perhaps tick the right boxes but have nothing personal in them. This is what I call Hallmark speaking. Hallmark cards sell because you can use the same card and give it to many different people. Their messages are general enough to be recognised, but not personal enough to exclude people. But if your speech is so general that many different people could give it and it would be appropriate, you are in trouble!

Your speaking needs to be relevant to the audience you are speaking to. They need to feel that it is of significance to them—that their self-interest is addressed. Tell a personal story or one that is personal to that team or group. Speak about something that is part of their daily reality. Don't be bland and impersonal.

Craig Valentine refers to the 'unpleasant pleasantries,' comments like 'I want to thank you for the privilege of being here. It is an honour to be in your city. The weather is great!' No one really cares! Rather substitute that with a strong opening that captures their attention, that makes them sit up and take notice. You can end with thanks, so save it and start instead by going straight into a personal story that will make the audience more likely to tune in to you. The more compelling you can be at the start of your speaking, the more chance you won't be speaking to yourself with no one else paying attention!

A simple technique when making your speaking more personal, is to use the word 'you' frequently. Your audience is more likely to respond to a statement that includes 'you' and 'your.' rather than 'we' and 'all of us.' Keep concepts as personal as possible, which will increase your audience engagement significantly.

Personal calls, messages, and emails offer you an opportunity to validate. What has that person or team done that is commendable? How have they contributed to the greater team? Take a moment to reflect on this before you call. We are far more likely to criticise than we are to compliment. When you are the one to constantly find reasons to validate people, you are more likely to be the one who connects when speaking.

Respond Personally to Criticism and Compliments

There may be times when you are criticised, but you can take the opportunity to connect by keeping it personal. My approach is to immediately personally respond to emails that criticise me or that are critical of events or people. The sooner you respond, the better. (If you are upset at the criticism, give yourself time and space to calm down first before responding). If possible, I call the person who sent me the email. This allows me to make them feel heard and to ask any questions I have. The important thing is to listen far more than you talk at this point. Giving a critic the time, the respect, and the space to have their say is powerful. Usually making the person feel heard dissipates the tension. Your call to your critic is an act of validation. Your call demonstrates that you honour their opinion and are willing to hear them out.

Depending on your personality, your next step will vary. If you are quite volatile, you might want to end the call there and say you need time to think things over. You would then wait, process, and respond when you are in a calmer frame of mind. Do not react in anger—that has a much higher chance of ending badly. Respond when you are calm enough to respond rather than react. If you are more even-tempered, you might be able to respond appropriately on the spot. Most of us benefit from time to process and to think before we respond. Give yourself time to respond in a way that is positive and that isn't risky for you. Set yourself up to respond when you are at your best rather than when you are angry.

There may also be many occasions when someone compliments you on something you have done. When someone takes the time and trouble to send you a compliment, personally thank them. Tell them how you feel receiving that compliment. Your expressing your appreciation validates them. There is nothing worse than complimenting someone and then not receiving a response. Resist the temptation to reciprocate with a compliment of your own—rather create a separate opportunity to validate that person. I recently heard someone saying: "I like your shoes". The immediate response was: "Thank you. I like your shoes too". That is not necessary and comes across as insincere. Simply say thank you.

How to Build your Influence and Presence

I have learned that we generally underestimate our own personal presence and influence. This was first brought to my attention when I was leading a big team. Previous leaders had discovered that personal calls made by senior leaders in the organisation delivered results.

These calls were never decrees or orders to do certain tasks. The calls only worked if the person making the call was authentic, personal, and positive. My approach was always to introduce myself first and ask if it was convenient to talk. If so, I would always ask them how life as a regional manager, for example, was treating them. This was my opportunity to tune in to that person. I gained valuable clues to their current challenges, attitudes, and capacity to attend to their duties. Simply by listening, I gained valuable insights and points of connection that helped me understand how to manage the conversation.

A call from someone more senior than you can be a powerful motivator, but only if the person making the call is positive and encouraging. If you are making the call, your agenda is to get that person on your side—doing what needs to be done and being motivated to support the greater team. Your challenge is to connect with them personally, and then to motivate and inspire them to take action. This process is as valid for volunteers as it is for staff within the organisation. Your ability to keep it personal will to a large extent determine whether you'll be the one to speak, connect and succeed.

Speak, Connect and Succeed
The Process of Keeping it Personal

Use Names as often as Possible—make it a habit. It shows you care, and it makes you stand out. We all thrive on personal recognition.

Personalise your Messages and Emails—take the time to make them personal. Speak to the self-interest of the person or team you are addressing.

Personal Phone Calls are Powerful—one phone call from you is more effective than multiple messages and emails. Connect personally, not digitally, to get the best results.

Hallmark Cards work because they are generic and applicable to many different people. Your speaking should be the opposite—personalised to those you are addressing. Be specific to the occasion and to the group you are addressing.

Respond Personally to Criticism and Compliments—the worst thing you can do is to refuse to respond. There is power in responding personally and quickly to criticism. Compliments also deserve a personal response.

Build your Influence and Presence by keeping your speaking personal. It's a vital component to being the one to speak and connect.

Once you start making a habit of keeping your speaking personal, you'll be astounded at the difference this one technique can make. As you become aware of the power of keeping it personal, you will notice that very few people have mastered this skill. From this point onwards, you will come across multiple opportunities every day to personalise your speaking.

When you do this regularly, you will become aware that you connect more powerfully with those that you're speaking to. Your ability to influence, persuade and build your reputation will be enhanced when you keep your conversations personal. That is a huge amount of reward for a very simple technique!

Chapter 8

Speak, Connect and Succeed
In times of Conflict

Conflict is a part of daily life. Chances are that you deal with conflict every single day from having to negotiate traffic, waiting in line for your lunch order, or sitting around a table with your family for a meal. Conflict can be very unpleasant, distracting, and exhausting. At times, it comes at great cost and can even ruin relationships—both personal and professional. But conflict can also be positive. If managed well, conflict can clear up misunderstandings and help us plot the way forward. You can speak, connect and succeed in times of conflict by using these techniques. View conflict as yet another opportunity to build and enhance your reputation and influence.

Be Aware of your Own Agenda

How you speak up in times of conflict can add to the conflict or help to diffuse it. You need to be aware of your personal agenda when you speak. What is your relationship to the conflict? Do you want or need to be right? Why is that so important to you? Do you have the habit of always needing to have the last word? Do you want to use the conflict to show up someone else's mistakes? Do you consider the conflict to be temporary or permanent? Are you perhaps enjoying the conflict? Do you actually want to resolve the conflict, or does the conflict serve you on some level? Your answers to these questions will determine how you speak up and whether or not you will stand out. It goes without saying that you want to be the one to stand out for the right reasons.

My own attitude and preference is that conflict should always be temporary. I'll work towards resolving conflict so that things can go back to being normal. I prefer to deal with conflict as quickly as possible, so that it allows everyone to move on in a positive way. We all manage conflict and react to it in different ways. Mostly, I can deal with conflict without 'losing it.' Other days, I don't manage it that well. Usually I can make my point in a calm manner, without raising my voice. Being shouted at never helps me resolve conflict, and neither will shouting at others. Talking, listening to one another, and working towards a solution are the steps that help me to resolve conflict. In my experience, conflict is never resolved by email.

A key question to ask yourself and the other parties involved is 'How have I contributed towards the conflict?' Often our ways of contributing are subtle—we can say something or choose not to respond. We can spot a problem, knowing it will escalate, and decide not to draw attention to it. We can keep the conflict going, even after we have apparently worked to resolve it. We may actually enjoy the conflict and love saying what we know we will have to apologise for later. All these actions reflect our personal agenda with regard to conflict. If we are honest with ourselves, we all play many more games than we would admit to.

What we don't always like to examine is the impact of the conflict. This impact can demoralise a team, distract them from their work, or make them completely dysfunctional. Relationships often don't recover from conflict, which can erode trust to the point of no return. Conflict can have a financial cost—you could end up losing key staff members, contracts, or your reputation. Take a moment to analyse the conflict you are dealing with, the impact or cost of that conflict, and your contribution to it. Once you have done that, you will be in a better position to plan how you can possibly speak, connect and succeed in times of conflict.

Here are some principles that will help you stand out when you speak up in times of conflict:

Focus on the Issues, not the People

Focus on the issues, not the people. Let's face it—you probably know someone who irritates you simply by breathing! There will always be difficult personalities to deal with and people that push all our buttons. Our challenge is to focus on the issues—if we can succeed with this, then we can navigate the treacherous waters of conflict. Personal attacks simply increase the conflict exponentially. Our natural response to a personal attack is to go on the offensive and respond in kind. In this way, conflict that is not well managed will escalate quickly. You cannot always manage someone else's reaction to conflict, but you can be accountable for how you react.

Examine your Own Reaction

Take a moment to think—what is the real issue? I learned a valuable lesson about myself during a conflict. I like to be very prepared for an event. I plan ahead of time and pay careful attention to detail. At one point I had organised an event and sent out communications to 60 people inviting them to attend. Another person on my team called me shortly before the event to question the choice of venue. He suggested that I find a better venue and communicate the changes to everyone involved. (I had not personally seen the venue and relied upon another team member to make the choice on my behalf.) After we debated the matter at some length, I eventually lost my temper and refused to change the venue.

What I discovered in hindsight (such a wonderful perspective to have!), was that the conflict was not actually about the venue at all. I seldom lose my temper, and my extreme reaction was the result of one of my core values being challenged. I was unaware that one of my core values was being very prepared well ahead of time. I didn't want last minute changes, as in my head, this reflected badly on me. The other person was focused on having a professional event. He was unafraid of last-minute changes. My strong objection was the clue I needed to learn this about myself. I have to admit that the venue wasn't what I was expecting, and I should have listened and changed it. I did apologise!

Examine your own reaction to conflict, remember that often the real issue is not the issue being discussed. If you can identify the trigger, you are more likely to be able to step back and respond in a more rational, less emotional way. Stephen Covey said: 'The main thing is to keep the main thing the main thing.' Our triggers are sometimes more obvious to others than to ourselves. If you find yourself continually reacting strongly to conflict, take a moment to assess what your triggers are. If you can make that link, you are in a better position to manage yourself. If you are not sure what your triggers are, ask those close to you. They will probably be able to identify them more easily than you can. At this point, remember to go into listen-only mode. Don't react and become defensive. Simply listen and give the matter some thought. This insight is so valuable—take the time to make the links.

If you are volatile by nature, create time to respond rather than to react. Give yourself time to blow off steam before you respond. Even in face-to-face situations, ask for time to process what is being discussed. Buying this time gives you an opportunity to think and process before responding. When I faced situations when I was very stressed and angry, I turned to two of my mentors. I arranged to meet and asked their permission to vent my frustrations. I knew I could speak to them in confidence. They were experienced leaders who were able to give me a perspective that I wouldn't have had on my own. They provided me with a safe space to channel my anger. Then they gave me advice that helped me go back to the situation as an adult, not as a toddler throwing a temper tantrum. I will forever be grateful for this support.

Choose your venting partner carefully. This person needs to be able to add value and give you perspective. We can easily find someone who will side with us and blame the other person, but that is not helpful. You need advice that will help you resolve the conflict, not perpetuate it. You want to come away with a different perspective—one that makes it easier for you to deal with conflict.

Always remind yourself of the bigger picture. What is the context in which this conflict is happening? What is your part in the whole? How does this conflict impact you, your team or your company? What is the cost of keeping this conflict going? Is there a cost when one person insists on being right?

Who's Watching which Movie?

One of the best techniques I was shown to defuse my own reaction to conflict came from a colleague, Erich. I called him one day to ask for advice on dealing with conflict. I will never forget his words. He advised me to approach the conflict with empathy, which was not what I wanted to hear. I wanted to respond with anger, but he put it to me this way: 'Remember that the movie going on inside that person's head makes perfect sense to him.' Most people don't wake up determined to ruin your day. (Yes—there may be a few exceptions to this rule.) The person you are in conflict with is probably just as passionate and talented as you are. His or her perspective is simply different.

When people disagree with us, we often take it personally. We read purely fictional meanings into words and actions. We do this to support the narrative and movie that is going on in our head. If we are honest with ourselves, we would admit that we are adding drama to the situation. Take a deep breath, take another one, and step back. Write down what is really going on. Do a brain dump of what is going on inside your head. Then go through what you have written and separate the emotion from the facts. Focus on the facts: the process and the issue that is at the heart of the conflict. Then plan your response to that. One of the best books I have read that helped me manage my own reactions is *Loving what Is* by Byron Katie. She takes you through a process to examine your approach to a problem. This process is simple, yet profound. It works!

Look for a Win-Win

If your purpose is to resolve the conflict, then strive to reach a win-win agreement. If the solution is a win-lose, then resentments will inevitably follow. You can choose words that make it easier to reach a win-win, such as remembering to always acknowledge contributions, even if they are contrary to your personal point of view. Acknowledging the emotion or passion from someone else is also a powerful way of diffusing the situation. Acknowledging the impact of the conflict on the parties involved is essential.

I've had to make peace with the fact that conflict is often only resolved temporarily. This is especially true when the source of the conflict is a clash of personalities. I've also had to learn to accept my limitations. I can only be responsible for my part in conflict and my own reaction. If others choose to perpetuate conflict, then that's their decision. We all default to certain behaviours, even when we try to guard against that. The skills you develop to resolve conflict will be well-used, as conflict rears its head far more frequently than we would like. If you can be the calm voice of reason in conflict, you'll be way ahead of most people. When your voice is the one that helps to resolve conflict in a positive way, you'll stand out when you speak up.

Speak, Connect and Succeed
Steps to Resolving Conflict

Be Aware of your own Agenda.
Do you want the conflict to be resolved? Why? Does it serve you in any way? How does this conflict impact you? What impact does it have on your team? What is the cost of the conflict?

Focus on the Issues, not the People.
Work towards identifying the real issues and the triggers that ignite the conflict.

Be Aware of your Reaction.
What buttons are being pressed? Which of your core values are being challenged?

Who's Watching which Movie?
Be aware of another viewpoint to your own. Have empathy. Strive to replace anger with empathy.

Look for a Win-Win.
Look for creative ways to move forward in a positive manner. Acknowledge opposing points of view and emotions.

Conflict comes in many different forms and at many different times. This reality provides us with many opportunities to hone our skills with regard to speaking up in times of conflict. Being calm, focusing on the real issues, and being aware of your reactions will help you. Remember to strive to respond rather than to react without thinking. Adding empathy and working towards not always needing to be right will help you manage your own reaction, as well as the conflict itself.

There will be times you get this right, so take some time to congratulate yourself on managing a difficult situation well. If you don't manage yourself well, try and understand what triggers you reacted to. Mentally replay the situation to understand where you could have responded differently and more effectively. Keep referring to these techniques to remind yourself of your approach.

Chapter 9

The Conversation with Yourself

The conversation with yourself is the only one that is invisible - a conversation that only you can participate in and hear. However, the consequences of your self-talk are visible on many levels, from your level of self-confidence, to how calm and assertive you are, to how you are able to connect with others.

The conversation we have most often, even incessantly, is the one that we have with ourselves. This happens without our necessarily being aware of it. As it's so pervasive in our everyday life, it is an important conversation to examine. It doesn't make sense to strive to speak and connect positively when speaking to others if you ignore those techniques when talking to yourself! As with any other conversation, our self–talk, the conversation inside our own head should have a purpose. Do yourself a favour—pretend you are an outsider listening in on the self-talk that is going on inside your head. Make a note of how often the self-talk is positive and how often it is negative.

You might be shocked to realize how rude you are talking to yourself! If you spoke to a colleague like that, would you still have a job? If you spoke to your friends in the same way, would you still have any friends? I try to make it a habit to say something positive to myself everytime I look in the mirror. Compliment yourself—cheer yourself on. Stop fixating on those looks that you wish you could change. Make peace with the fact that you are unlikely to ever be on the cover of *Vogue* magazine!

My point is this: your self-talk sets the stage for all other conversations you have with those around you. If your self-talk is constantly negative, it's hard to be the person who speaks positively to others. If you cannot validate yourself, can you validate others? You should be your own biggest fan. Just as it is important to validate others, you need to validate yourself. I find that when I am generous in my validation of my own efforts, it allows me to relax. If I am always telling myself what I am doing wrong, it puts me on edge. Negative self-talk becomes a filter through which I see those around me. In my opinion, people who constantly put others down often have low self-esteem. Those who continually validate others come from a place of quiet confidence in their own abilities. That is the head-space that you should strive to be in. That is a head-space from which positive possibilities grow.

The good news is that irrespective of the point at which you are starting from, you can change. Staying positive is a process and a habit, not an event. Just like plants need to be watered regularly to thrive, you need to have a constant stream of positive energy to be at your best. What I have found most helpful is to constantly have positive thoughts, energy and material coming into my head-space. I achieve that by choosing my reading material very carefully. The same goes for what I watch on TV and listen to on the radio. My family often shake their heads when I walk away from very violent TV shows. My attitude is that my time is precious—why would I watch something that depresses and upsets me? I would far rather walk away and go and read, watch, or listen to something that leaves me feeling uplifted and positive. Some of my personal favourite positive shots of energy include the 'Notes from the Universe,' written by Mike Dooley. These personalised, quirky, positive messages come into my inbox every weekday. Read inspiring books or listen to TED Talks or podcasts that resonate with you.

Another way I de-stress is to exercise. For me, going for a run is one way to ground myself and get back to normal. I am fortunate to live near to Kirstenbosch Botanical Gardens in Cape Town. If I am struggling with issues, I go and walk there. Spending time there in a beautiful environment calms me and helps me gain perspective. What do you do to nurture yourself? Do it often. The more grounded and relaxed you are, the better your chance to speak, connect and succeed.

What is the purpose of the conversation you are having with yourself? Your purpose should be to validate, uplift, and motivate yourself. Catch yourself doing something right. Of course we all deliver far from stellar performances sometimes, but the important thing is to determine what defines you. Do not allow your occasional mistakes and errors of judgment to define you. A bad day doesn't have to become your norm. We all have bad days. I can think of many instances where my speaking up allowed me to stand out for the wrong reasons. But life is not static. It takes many twists and turns, so don't focus on your worst day and keep reminding yourself of what you did wrong, what opportunities you missed, and how you embarrassed yourself. Deliberately review the days when you spoke up and stood out. Take a moment to pat yourself on the back and realise the impact you had or the results you achieved. Remind yourself of the days when you made a difference or when someone complimented you on your contribution. Choose to allow those positive days to define you.

My children often tease me about my reading habits. I love self-help books. I am curious by nature, and I love to constantly learn and try to improve myself. From my library of self-help books, I have found two techniques that I use constantly. The first is to practice expressing gratitude and the second is to visualize the outcome that I am working towards. I recently came across this beautiful quote by Melody Beattie: 'Gratitude unlocks the fullness of life. It turns what we have into enough and more. It turns denial into acceptance, chaos to order, confusion to clarity. It can turn a meal into a feast, a house into a home, a stranger into a friend.'

Whenever I have a moment to spare, I look around me and give thanks for what I have. By appreciating all that you normally take for granted, you immediately put yourself into a more positive frame of mind. This allows me to operate from a more positive space. When you are positive, you have more to give—to a project, to a colleague, to your team. Like attracts like, so the more positive you are, the more likely you are to find other positive people to work with.

I also make a habit of giving thanks in advance, by making a statement of how I would like a meeting to go or how a person will react to my suggestions. Think of this as a game entitled *If I could write the script, this is what would happen.* If I am submitting a proposal to a client, I mentally visualize the meeting going well and the client loving my ideas. I write the script and give thanks in advance that I'm able to answer all their questions confidently and position myself as a service provider who is the perfect match for their needs.

I give thanks that this meeting will have a positive conclusion. You may be surprised to learn that this is really effective. I suspect its power lies in changing my own attitude. When I go into a meeting with a clear picture and expectation in my mind as to the outcome, my speaking will be more focused and purposeful.

Visualizing the positive outcome I am working towards often helps me approach a problem. Your approach to a challenging situation will be vastly different when you go in saying to yourself, "I hope this doesn't end in confrontation" compared to "Thank you that everyone listened and was open to working together." Spending a few minutes visualizing the positive outcome you are looking for is vital. It's simply another way of preparing to speak, connect and succeed. You are mentally rehearsing the purpose and positive outcome of your conversation.

I have encountered many clients who spend far more time rehearsing their anxiety as opposed to rehearsing their presentation. I encourage them to spend time every day rehearsing the positive outcome of their presentation. Create a movie in your head. Imagine the room or environment you are speaking in. Imagine the conversation going well, where you are confident, articulate, and relaxed. Whoever you are speaking to really connects with you and what you are saying. You can tell your audience is engaged and is responding positively.

You are so grateful that you are well-prepared for this conversation or presentation! You leave with a specific call to action that others respond to. People walk up to you afterwards to thank you for your contribution. Your speaking made a difference. This technique is deceptively simple, but incredibly powerful. It's easy to master and will deliver tangible results.

Perhaps this chapter should have been the first chapter of this book. However it is often easier to understand and grasp techniques that involve other people. Once you understand these, it is easier to then apply them to yourself. Your speaking can and will allow you to be the one to speak, connect and succeed.

Conclusion

Whatever you do in life, your ability to speak, connect and succeed will be a catalyst for opportunity. Every Facebook post, Tweet, email, or instant message you send is your voice speaking. You and I have multiple opportunities every day to choose how we speak.

What do you want to be known for? What do you want people to remember about you? How can your speaking contribute to your ambitions and dreams?

This book has shown you practical ways to build your reputation every time you speak. These skills work and will enhance your presence and influence. Simply by being more purposeful and intentional, you can make your speaking more meaningful. The impact of your speaking can be profound. Your words can inspire and motivate. Just as easily, your words can be hurtful and destructive. You can build relationships through your speaking or destroy them. The choice is yours. Today, this minute, this hour.

Buying this book is an investment in yourself. Applying the teaching of this book will deliver a profound return on that investment. Read this book again. Constantly challenge yourself to keep making progress. Join Toastmasters—your membership will accelerate this process. Remember to be kind to yourself and to make the conversation with yourself a positive one.

Speaking is something we do innately—often without thinking.
The consequences of our spoken words are profound.
Your speaking can change the mood of a room, and it can inspire someone to believe in his ability.
Your words can open up opportunities for you to en-

hance your reputation.

Just as easily, your words can showcase your vulnerabilities or ruin your day.

As you speak, you can engineer your future career prospects, or engineer your swift exit.

Your speaking will identify which kind of leader you are and whether or not people want you on their team.

Your speaking will determine whether or not you stand out from the crowd.

When you master the art of speaking purposefully and powerfully, doors will open up for you that you never imagined were within your reach. This book has set you on a journey that will deliver results, that will enhance your prospects.

Go and build your reputation every time you speak.

Congratulations! You have made it to the end of Speak, Connect, Succeed. The time and energy you spent reading this book will give you a very powerful return on investment. You already have what it takes to be successful. By enhancing your ability to use everyday conversations to connect and succeed, you multiply the opportunities for you to be noticed (for the right reasons!). In the process, you will build your reputation and increase your influence. Our world needs people like you to stand out when you speak up. We need inspirational leaders and speakers. We need you to speak to us, connect with us, and to inspire us. Whatever you are passionate about, there are people around you who need to hear your story and your message. My hope is that you will become one of many who will speak up effectively. In the process your voice will contribute to a better world, where our conversations add value and benefit all of us. I look forward to hearing your message and seeing the impact that you'll have on those around you!

Let's Continue the Conversation

Thank you for reading my book! Your opinion matters to me.

I would be grateful if you would leave a review on www.amazon.com for me. Much of the content of this book has been enriched by listening to the opinions and comments of others. I would love your voice to be heard as well.

If you are interested in my keynote speaking, workshops or coaching, simply send me an email to aletta@voicingyourpotential.com to set up a call.

Have you dreamed of publishing your own book? This book was half-written for many years. It was only when I enrolled at Self-Publishing School that this book became a reality for me. If you would like to find out more, and find out how to go from blank page to published author in 90 days, follow this link:
https://xe172.isrefer.com/go/sps4fta-vts/bookbrosinc3133

www.ingramcontent.com/pod-product-compliance
Lightning Source LLC
Chambersburg PA
CBHW071214220526
45468CB00002B/598